# READ THIS!

## Fascinating Stories from the Content Areas

Daphne Mackey
& Alice Savage

**2**

CAMBRIDGE UNIVERSITY PRESS
Cambridge, New York, Melbourne, Madrid, Cape Town,
Singapore, São Paulo, Delhi, Mexico City

Cambridge University Press
32 Avenue of the Americas, New York, NY 10013-2473, USA

www.cambridge.org
Information on this title: www.cambridge.org/9780521747899

First published 2010
6th printing 2012

Printed in Hong Kong, China, by Golden Cup Printing Company Limited

*A catalog record for this publication is available from the British Library.*

*Library of Congress Cataloging-in-Publication Data*

Mackey, Daphne.
Read this! 2 : fascinating stories from the content areas / Daphne Mackey, Alice Savage.
p. cm.
ISBN 978-0-521-74789-9 (pbk. : Student's bk.) — ISBN 978-0-521-74791-2 (pbk. : Teacher's manual)
1. English language — Textbooks for foreign speakers. 2. Interdisciplinary approach in education. I. Savage, Alice,
1962- II. Title. III. Title: Fascinating stories from the content areas.

PE1128.M3243 2010
428.6'4—dc22

2010003376

ISBN 978-0-521-74789-9 Student's Book
ISBN 978-0-521-74791-2 Teacher's Manual

Art direction, book design, layout services, and photo research: Adventure House, NYC
Audio production: Paul Ruben Productions

# Contents

# Introduction

## ABOUT THE SERIES

*Read This!* is a three-level reading series for high beginning, low intermediate, and intermediate-level English learners. The series is designed to enhance students' confidence and enjoyment of reading in English, build their reading skills, and develop their vocabulary.

The readings in the series are high interest and content-rich. They are all nonfiction and contain fascinating true information. The style of writing makes the information easily digestible, and the language is carefully controlled at each level to make the texts just challenging enough, but easily accessible.

Each book in *Read This!* consists of five thematically related units. Each unit is loosely connected to a different academic discipline that might be studied in an institution of higher education, such as business, engineering, psychology, health care, or mathematics. Each unit is divided into three chapters, and each chapter contains a reading accompanied by exercise material. Besides the main theme of the unit, each chapter is tied to a secondary academic content area so that students can experience an interdisciplinary approach to a topic.

Accompanying each reading is a variety of pre- and postreading activities. They are designed to provide a balance of reading comprehension, vocabulary, and reading skill development. Many activities also provide opportunities for student discussion and a chance for students to connect the topics of the readings to their own lives and experience. Each unit ends with a wrap-up that reviews ideas and vocabulary from all three chapters of the unit.

Vocabulary instruction is an important focus of *Read This!* Selected words from each reading are previewed, presented, practiced, and recycled. These words are drawn from the two academic disciplines that are brought together in each reading. In addition, selected words from the Academic Word List (AWL) are pulled out from each reading for instruction.

Each unit is designed to take 6–9 hours of class time, depending on how much out-of-class work is assigned by the teacher. The units can either be taught in the order they appear or out of sequence. It is also possible to teach the chapters within a unit out of order. However, by teaching the units and chapters in sequence, students will benefit fully from the presentation, practice, and recycling of the target vocabulary.

All the readings in the *Read This!* series have been recorded for those students whose language learning can be enhanced by listening to a text as well as by reading it. However, since the goal of the series is to build students' readings skills, students should be told to read and study the texts without audio before they choose to listen to them.

The audio files can be found on the *Read This!* Web site at www.cambridge.org/readthis. Students can go to this site and listen to the audio recordings on their computers, or they can download the audio recordings onto their personal MP3 players to listen to them at any time.

An audio CD of the readings is also available in the back of each Teacher's Manual for those teachers who would like to bring the recorded readings into their classroom for students to hear. Also in the Teacher's Manual are photocopiable unit tests.

## THE UNIT STRUCTURE

### Unit Opener

The title, at the top of the first page of each unit, names the academic content area that unifies the three chapters in the unit. The title of each chapter also appears, along with a picture and a short blurb that hints at the content of the chapter reading. These elements are meant to intrigue readers and whet their appetites for what is to come. At the bottom of the page, the main academic content area of the unit is repeated, and the secondary academic content area for each chapter is given as well.

### 1 Topic Preview

The opening page of each chapter includes a picture and two tasks: Part A and Part B. Part A is usually a problem-solving task in which students are asked to bring some of their background knowledge or personal opinions to bear. Part B always consists of three discussion questions that draw students closer and closer to an idea of what the reading is about. In fact, the last question, *What do you think the reading is going to be about?* is always the same in every chapter: This is to help learners get into the habit of predicting what texts will be about before they read.

### 2 Vocabulary Preview

This section has students preview selected words that appear in the reading. It contains two tasks: Part A and Part B. Part A presents selected words for the students to study and learn. Part B has the students check their understanding of these words.

In Part A, the selected words are listed in three boxes. The box on the left contains words that relate to the main content area of the unit. The box on the right contains words that relate to the secondary content area of the reading. Between these two boxes are words from the reading that come from the Academic Word List (AWL). Placing the AWL words between the two lists of content area words creates a visual representation of the fact that the content area words are specific to separate content areas, while the AWL words are general academic words that might appear in either content area.

Note that the part of speech of a word is given in the chart only if this word could also be a different part of speech. Also note that some words are accompanied by words in parentheses. This alerts students to some common collocations that can form with the word and that will appear in the reading.

The vocabulary in the Vocabulary Preview is recycled over and over. The words appear in the reading; in Section 5, Vocabulary Check; in the Unit Wrap-Ups; and in the unit tests.

## 3 Reading

This section contains the reading and one or two pieces of art that illustrate it. Some words from the reading are glossed at the bottom of the page. These are low-frequency words that students are not expected to know. Understanding these words might be important for understanding the reading; however, it would probably not be useful for students to incorporate the words into their active vocabulary.

The icon at the top of the page indicates that the reading is available as an MP3 file online. Students can access this by going to the *Read This!* Web site at www.cambridge.org/readthis.

## 4 Reading Check

This section is designed to check students' comprehension of the text. Part A checks their understanding of the main ideas. Part B asks students to retrieve more detailed information from the reading.

## 5 Vocabulary Check

In this section, students revisit the same vocabulary that they studied before they read the text and that they have since encountered in the reading. The Vocabulary Check contains two tasks: Part A and Part B. In Part A, students are asked to complete a text by choosing appropriate vocabulary words for the context. The text in Part A is essentially a summary of the most salient information in the reading. This activity both reinforces the target vocabulary for the chapter and the content of the reading.

Part B varies from chapter to chapter. Sometimes it has a game-like quality, where students have to unscramble a word or find the odd word out in a group of words. Sometimes the task helps students extend their understanding of the target words by working with other parts of speech derived from the words. Other times, the task tests students' knowledge of other words that the target words often co-occur with (their collocations).

## 6 Applying Reading Skills

An important strand of *Read This!* is reading skill development. Students are introduced to a variety of skills, such as finding main ideas and supporting details, inferencing, identifying cause and effect, and organizing information from a reading into a chart. Practicing these skills will help students gain a deeper understanding of the content of the reading and the author's purpose. The section opens with a brief explanation of the reading skill and why it is important.

This section has two tasks: Part A and Part B. In Part A, students usually work with some kind of graphic organizer that helps them practice the skill and organize information. This work will prepare them to complete Part B.

## 7 Discussion

This section contains at least three questions that will promote engaging discussion and encourage students to connect the ideas and information in the readings to their own knowledge and experience. Many of the questions take students beyond the readings. There is also ample opportunity for students to express their opinions. This section helps students consolidate their understanding of the reading and use the target vocabulary from the chapter.

## WRAP-UP

Each unit ends with a Wrap-Up, which gives students the chance to review vocabulary and ideas from the unit. It will also help them prepare for the unit test. (The photocopiable unit tests are to be found in the Teacher's Manual.) Teachers may want to pick and choose which parts of the Wrap-Up they decide to have students do, since to do all the activities for every unit might be overly time-consuming. The Wrap-Up section consists of the following:

Vocabulary Review. All the target vocabulary from the three chapters of the unit is presented in a chart. The chart is followed by an activity in which students match definitions to some of the words in the chart.

Vocabulary in Use. Students engage in mini-discussions in which they use some of the target language from the unit. Students will be able to draw on their personal experience and knowledge of the world.

Role Play. Students work with the concepts of the readings by participating in a structured and imaginative oral activity. The role plays require that the students have understood and digested the content of at least one of the readings in a chapter. One advantage of role plays is that they are self-leveling. In other words, the sophistication of the role play is determined by the level and oral proficiency of the students. Students will need help in preparing for the role plays. They will also need time to prepare for them. It might be a good idea for the teacher to model the first role play with one of the stronger students in the class.

Writing. This section of the Wrap-Up provides the teacher with an opportunity to have students do some writing about the content of the unit. The setup of this section varies from unit to unit.

WebQuest. For those students, programs, or classrooms that have Internet access, students can log onto www.cambridge.org/readthis. They can then find the WebQuest for the unit that they have been studying. The WebQuest is essentially an Internet scavenger hunt in which students retrieve information from Web sites that they are sent to. In this way, students encounter the information from the chapters once more. The Web sites confirm what they have already read and then broaden their knowledge of the unit topics by leading them to additional information. The WebQuests may be done individually or in pairs. Students may either submit their answers to the teacher online or they can print out a completed answer sheet and hand it in to the teacher.

# Acknowledgments

Many people have been involved in the development, writing, and editing of *Read This! 2*. We would especially like to thank Bernard Seal for bringing us into the project. His involvement in the series and his knowledge of the field have helped at every step.

Our editor, Angela Castro, and in-house senior development editor, Kathleen O'Reilly, have done an outstanding job of keeping us on track. Thanks, too, to the associate development editor, Caitlin Mara; the production editor, Heather McCarron; the copyeditor, Sylvia Bloch; and the fact checker, Mandie Drucker.

Special thanks go to Averil Coxhead for permission to cite from the Academic Word List (AWL). For the most up-to-date information on the AWL, go to http://www.victoria.ac.nz/lals/resources/academicwordlist.

We are grateful to the reviewers, whose comments and suggestions were most helpful: John Bunting, Georgia State University; Mohammed Etedali, Kuwait; Devra Miller, San Mateo Unified High School District; Wendy Ramer, Broward Community College; Hsin Yi Shen, Taiwan; and Kerry Vrabel, Gateway Community College.

Daphne would like to thank her co-author, Alice Savage. She has been a delight to work with, contributing creativity and humor. Daphne would also like to thank her colleagues and students at the University of Washington for their enthusiasm and dedication, and George and Caroline for their patience with her writing habit.

Alice would like to thank Daphne for her steady nerves and skill with a pen. Alice is also grateful to her colleagues and the students of Lone Star College, North Harris. It's a great place to work and learn. She would also like to thank her family: Masoud, Cyrus, and Kaveh. They make home a great place to play!

Daphne Mackey
Alice Savage

UNIT

# 1

# Health Care

## Chapter 1

### The World's Best-Selling Medicine

Felix Hoffmann wanted to help his father. What followed was one of the biggest success stories in business.

**Content areas:**
- Health Care
- Business

## Chapter 2

### Fighting Disease with Disease

A doctor in a farming community made a discovery that has saved millions of lives.

**Content areas:**
- Health Care
- History

## Chapter 3

### Saved from Certain Death

Everyone expected Jeanna Giese to die, but one doctor did not give up.

**Content areas:**
- Health Care
- Science

## 1 TOPIC PREVIEW

**A** People have different ways to stop pain. Put a check (✓) next to ways you stop a headache. Share your answers with your classmates.

**1** _____ put ice on your head

**2** _____ go to sleep

**3** _____ take aspirin

**4** _____ take a medicine called " _____ "

**5** _____ _____ (your idea)

**B** Read the title of this chapter, look at the picture, and discuss the following questions.

**1** What do you think people did when they had a headache a thousand years ago? A hundred years ago?

**2** Can you name a best-selling medicine?

**3** What do you think the reading is going to be about?

## 2 VOCABULARY PREVIEW

**A** Read the word lists. Put a check (✓) next to the words that you know and can use in a sentence. Compare your answers with a partner. Then look up any unfamiliar words in a dictionary.

| Health Care | Academic Word List | Business |
| --- | --- | --- |
| fever<br>(be in) **pain**<br>patient<br>pill<br>prevent<br>**treat** (*v.*) | researcher<br>similar | company<br>manager<br>on the market<br>**produce** (*v.*) |

The chart shows selected words from the reading related to health care, business, and the Academic Word List (AWL). For more information about the AWL, see page 121.

**B** Write the word from Part A next to its definition.

1 The feeling when something hurts you: _____

2 The person who controls a business or the workers:

_____

3 To help someone who is sick: _____

4 A medical condition with higher than normal body temperature:

_____

5 Available for sale: _____

6 An organization that sells goods or services to make money:

_____

7 Medicine that is not liquid. You can pick it up and take it with water: _____

8 To stop something from happening: _____

9 Almost the same: _____

10 Someone who goes to see a doctor: _____

11 To make or create something: _____

12 A person who does a study to learn more about something:

_____

Preview the questions in Reading Check Part A on page 6. Then read the story.

# The World's Best-Selling Medicine

*Willow tree*

1    One of the biggest success stories in business comes from the world of medicine. It started with a man named Felix Hoffmann. Hoffmann's father was old and in a lot of pain. Hoffmann was a scientist, so he started looking for a way to help his father.

2    Since ancient times, people all over the world have used willow[1] to stop pain. The willow tree contains salicylic acid. This stops pain, but there is one problem. Salicylic acid also hurts the stomach. In 1853, a French scientist made a mixture from willow that did not hurt the stomach. However, his mixture was difficult to make, and he did not try to produce or sell it.

3    In 1897, in Germany, Hoffmann also made a mixture with salicylic acid. He tried it himself first and then gave it to his father. His father's pain went away, and the mixture did not hurt his stomach.

4    Hoffmann worked for Bayer, a German company. He showed his new drug to his manager, who tested the drug and found that it worked well. Bayer decided to make the drug. They called it *aspirin* and put the Bayer name on every pill.

---

[1] *willow:* a kind of tree with long branches that hang down

Aspirin was an immediate success. Almost everyone has pain of some kind, so aspirin answered a true need. Aspirin was cheap, easy to take, and effective. It also lowered fevers. Aspirin was a wonder drug.

At first, Bayer sold the drug through doctors, who then sold it to their patients. In 1915, the company started to sell aspirin in drugstores. In the United States, Bayer had a patent[2] on the drug. Other companies could make similar products and sell them in other countries, but only Bayer could make and sell aspirin in the United States. In time, Bayer could no longer own the name aspirin in the United States. Other companies could make it there, too. However, Bayer aspirin was the most well known, and for many years, it was the market leader.

By the 1950s, new painkillers were on the market. Aspirin was no longer the only way to treat pain and reduce fever. Bayer and other companies looked for other drugs to make. However, in the 1970s they got a surprise. Doctors noticed that patients who were taking aspirin had fewer heart attacks[3] than other people. A British researcher named John Vane found the reason aspirin helped to prevent heart attacks. In 1982, he won the Nobel Prize[4] for his research. Doctors started to tell some of their patients to take aspirin every day to prevent heart attacks.

Aspirin bottle, 1899

This new use gave new life to sales of aspirin. In the United States, people take about 80 million aspirin a day. In fact, aspirin is the world's best-selling medicine. Aspirin has been a great success. It has made life better for the many people who take it. It has also made a lot of money for companies like Bayer that produce and sell it!

[2] *patent:* a legal right to ownership of an invention
[3] *heart attack:* a serious medical condition in which the heart does not get enough blood, often causing death
[4] *Nobel Prize:* an international prize given each year to leaders in their fields

# 4 READING CHECK

**A** Are these statements true or false? Write *T* (true) or *F* (false).

1 _____ Salicylic acid stops headache pain.

2 _____ Hoffmann was the manager of a drug company.

3 _____ People today take aspirin for many reasons.

**B** Circle the letter of the best answer.

1 Why was Felix Hoffmann looking for a painkiller?
   **a** His father was in pain.
   **b** His company told him to do that.
   **c** He wanted to make a lot of money.

2 Why didn't the French scientist continue to make a medicine that stopped pain?
   **a** It didn't work well.
   **b** It hurt the stomach.
   **c** It was hard to make.

3 Why did Bayer start making aspirin?
   **a** because Hoffmann was working for them
   **b** because it helped prevent heart attacks
   **c** because other companies were making aspirin

4 What does *not* describe aspirin?
   **a** effective       **b** expensive       **c** easy to find in drugstores

5 Bayer aspirin was _____ .
   **a** the only drug with the name "aspirin"
   **b** not sold in the United States
   **c** the only aspirin sold in drugstores in 1915

6 When new painkillers came on the market, what happened to aspirin?
   **a** Fewer people bought it.
   **b** Companies stopped selling it.
   **c** Doctors sold it to patients.

7 Some people take one aspirin a day because they don't want to _____ .
   **a** get a cold       **b** have a heart attack       **c** have a stomachache

8 Aspirin makes money for drug companies because _____ .
   **a** it cures diseases       **b** it stops stomach pain       **c** so many people use it

# 5 VOCABULARY CHECK

**A** Retell the story. Fill in the blanks with the correct words from the box.

| | | | | |
|---|---|---|---|---|
| company | fevers | manager | on the market | pain |
| patients | pill | prevent | researcher | similar |

Felix Hoffmann's father was in a lot of _____ , so
Hoffmann did research and developed a mixture with salicylic acid.
It worked well. Hoffmann told his _____ at Bayer about
this. The _____ developed a drug called *aspirin*. It helped
stop pain and lower _____ . They tested the new drug and
found that it worked well. At first, Bayer sold aspirin only through doctors.
Then they made it in the form of a/an _____ and sold it
in drugstores.

By the 1950s, new painkillers came _____ .
These new drugs were _____ to aspirin. Then a/an
_____ found that aspirin helped to _____
heart attacks. Doctors began to tell some of their _____ to
take aspirin every day.

**B** Fill in the blanks with the correct form of the word.

| Verb | Noun |
|---|---|
| produce | product |
| research | researcher |
| treat | treatment |

**1** What is the best way to _____ a headache?

**2** Aspirin was a very successful _____ for Bayer.

**3** Bayer decided to _____ Hoffmann's drug.

**4** What is the usual _____ for a stomachache?

**5** Scientists began to _____ other uses for aspirin.

## 6 APPLYING READING SKILLS

> ***Understanding the order of events*** *in a reading means that you know what happens first, second, third, and so on. One way to check that you understand the order is to make a time line.*

**A** Put the following events into the time line in the correct order.

    **a** Other painkillers come onto the market to compete with Bayer.
    **b** John Vane's research shows aspirin can help prevent heart attacks.
    **c** A French scientist makes a painkiller from willow.
    **d** Bayer sells aspirin to doctors.
    **e** Bayer sells aspirin pills directly to drugstores.
    **f** Felix Hoffmann makes a painkiller from salicylic acid.
    **g** Hoffmann shows his new drug to his manager.

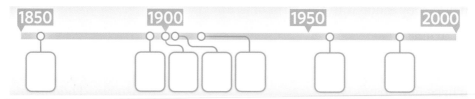

**B** Are these statements *T* (true) or *F* (false)? Use information from your time line in Part A and the reading to help you.

    **1** _____ A French scientist made a painkiller before Felix Hoffmann.

    **2** _____ Felix Hoffmann made a painkiller more than one hundred years ago.

    **3** _____ Bayer sold aspirin through drugstores before they sold it through doctors.

    **4** _____ Bayer sold less aspirin in the 1950s and 1960s than in the 1930s and 1940s.

    **5** _____ John Vane discovered a new use for aspirin after he won the Nobel Prize.

## 7 DISCUSSION

Discuss the following questions in pairs or groups.

    **1** What are some other common medical problems? How do you treat them?
    **2** Think of other medical products that have been successful. What makes a successful medical product? Why?
    **3** What new drug or medical product would you invent? What would it do?

# Fighting Disease with Disease

## 1 TOPIC PREVIEW

**A** Sometimes a disease moves quickly and affects a large group of people. One way that can happen is *through the air*. List three other ways a disease can move through a large group of people. Share your answers with your classmates.

**1** *through the air*

**2** _____

**3** _____

**4** _____

**B** Read the title of this chapter, look at the picture, and discuss the following questions.

**1** Have any diseases recently affected people where you live? Do you know how the diseases started?

**2** What year do you think it is in the picture? How do you think the picture relates to the subject of disease?

**3** What do you think the reading is going to be about?

## 2 VOCABULARY PREVIEW

**A** Read the word lists. Put a check (✓) next to the words that you know and can use in a sentence. Compare your answers with a partner. Then look up any unfamiliar words in a dictionary.

| Health Care | Academic Word List | History |
| --- | --- | --- |
| (find a) **cure** <br> epidemic <br> immune system <br> infection <br> vaccine <br> virus | challenge (*n.*) <br> method <br> (test a) **theory** | century <br> era <br> (in the) **late** ('20s/ '30s/etc.) |

The chart shows selected words from the reading related to health care, history, and the Academic Word List (AWL). For more information about the AWL, see page 121.

**B** Fill in the blanks with words from Part A.

**1** When most of the people in a city get sick, it is a/an _____ .

**2** My mother was born in the _____ 1960s.

**3** You should wash a cut so that you do not get a/an _____ .

**4** A/An _____ helps to prevent someone from getting a disease.

**5** The time between 1700 and 1799 is the 18th _____ .

**6** The doctor believed that the medicine would work, but it was only a/an _____ . He was not sure yet.

**7** Not all doctors do exactly the same thing. Sometimes a doctor has a different _____ for treating a disease.

**8** There was nothing doctors could do. No one was able to find a/an

_____ .

**9** A person who has a healthy _____ will not get sick easily.

**10** A/An _____ causes the common cold.

**11** It was a/an _____ for doctors to find a way to help the patient.

**12** In the _____ of the Internet, we often look online for medical information.

**3** READING

Preview the questions in Reading Check Part A on page 13. Then read the story.

# Fighting Disease with Disease

*Painting of Dr. Jenner giving a vaccination*

Cows have helped humans for thousands of years, but few people know about a special favor that we received from this animal. In fact, anyone who has ever had a vaccine to prevent a disease can thank cows and an English country doctor who lived more than 200 years ago.

In the late 1780s, a smallpox epidemic was killing thousands of people across Europe. Smallpox spreads through human contact. It starts with a fever. Then people get spots on their body. Many die. Others have scars[1] on their faces and bodies for the rest of their lives. Famous doctors and scientists could not find a cure for smallpox. During that era, they were beginning to use scientific methods to do experiments, but they did not understand the body's immune system and the way it worked.

Edward Jenner was a doctor in a small village in England. When smallpox began killing his patients, he tried to help. He asked a lot of questions, and he wrote down information about the disease. He talked to store owners, farmers, and teachers. People told him stories. They said that people who caught a disease called cowpox did not get smallpox.

Jenner decided to do scientific research on cowpox. He learned that people got cowpox from working with cows. It was not dangerous and

1

2

3

4

---

[1] *scar:* a mark left on the skin after an illness or injury

never killed anyone. The milkmaids[2] often got sick, but then they became healthy again and went back to work. Jenner did research, and he discovered that they did not get smallpox. The stories were true.

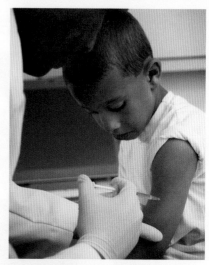

5    Jenner wanted to test the theory scientifically. He wanted to know what protected the milkmaids from infection. He decided to do an experiment. First, he infected a boy with cowpox. The boy got sick at first, but then he got better. Next, Dr. Jenner did a very dangerous thing. He infected the same boy with smallpox. Would the cowpox virus in the boy's body stop smallpox? Dr. Jenner thought so, but he did not know for sure.

6    Dr. Jenner and the boy's family watched the boy carefully for the next few days. Fortunately, Dr. Jenner's theory was correct. The boy did not get sick, and Dr. Jenner had found a way of stopping the smallpox epidemic. Dr. Jenner made one of the most important discoveries of the eighteenth century.

7    There was a new challenge, however. Dr. Jenner's ideas were very different from the way most doctors and scientists thought about medicine. They said, "How can you give a person one disease to stop them from getting another disease?" Jenner did many experiments to prove his theory. Finally, people saw that he was right.

8    Dr. Jenner decided to name his new treatment after the Latin for cow (*vacca*) and the Latin for cowpox (*vaccinia*). He called the treatment a *vaccination*. Doctors then started to vaccinate people, and the epidemic ended. There is still no cure for smallpox, but the smallpox vaccine prevents many people from getting this terrible disease.

9    Today, medical researchers are busy with new viruses. Disease specialists travel all over the world studying infectious diseases. They try to find vaccines to prevent these diseases. Their methods are similar to Dr. Jenner's. His idea of using one disease to fight another disease is still one of the main ways that scientists develop life-saving medicines.

---

[2] *milkmaids:* in earlier times, women who milked cows

# 4 READING CHECK

**A** Circle the letter of the best answer.

1 Where did the story take place?
   **a** France    **b** England    **c** the United States

2 What problem did people have?
   **a** hunger    **b** war    **c** disease

3 Who solved the problem?
   **a** a farmer    **b** a milkmaid    **c** a doctor

**B** Are these statements true or false? Write *T* (true) or *F* (false).

1 _____ The first vaccine was discovered 500 years ago.

2 _____ Milkmaids did not get smallpox.

3 _____ Only cows can get cowpox.

4 _____ Smallpox was more dangerous than cowpox.

5 _____ Dr. Jenner believed that cowpox might protect people from smallpox.

6 _____ Dr. Jenner infected himself with smallpox.

7 _____ Dr. Jenner infected a boy with smallpox. Then he infected the boy with cowpox.

8 _____ Dr. Jenner's experiment with the boy helped Jenner find a cure.

9 _____ Dr. Jenner named his medicine after the boy.

10 _____ At first, doctors did not believe Dr. Jenner, but they changed their minds later.

11 _____ A vaccine prevents people from getting a disease.

12 _____ There is a cure for smallpox.

## 5 VOCABULARY CHECK

**A** Retell the story. Fill in the blanks with the correct words from the box.

| | | | | |
|---|---|---|---|---|
| cure | epidemic | era | immune system | infected |
| late | method | theory | vaccine | virus |

Dr. Jenner lived in England in the _____ eighteenth

and early nineteenth centuries. It was a/an _____ when
                                                                    2

many people died of disease. When a smallpox _____ came
                                                                    3

through his town, many people went to him for help. He could not help them

because there was no _____ for smallpox.
                                          4

When Dr. Jenner learned that milkmaids did not get smallpox,

he developed a/an _____ about the disease. He
                              5

gave a boy cowpox. Then he _____ the boy with
                                                        6

the smallpox _____ . The cowpox helped the boy's
                              7

_____ , and the boy did not get smallpox. Dr. Jenner's
              8

_____ of doing research was unusual, but it was
              9

successful. He was able to create the first _____ .
                                                              10

**B** Use the clues to unscramble the words.

| | | | |
|---|---|---|---|
| **1** | _____ one hundred years | | tcryuen |
| **2** | _____ a difficult situation | | nehglacel |
| **3** | _____ something that causes disease | | uvrsi |
| **4** | _____ a period of time | | rae |
| **5** | _____ a way to do something | | dmeoth |
| **6** | _____ something that stops a disease | | ruec |

## 6 APPLYING READING SKILLS

> **Finding main ideas and supporting details** in a reading is an important skill. First, readers usually find the main ideas. Then good readers also look for details that support the main ideas.

**A** Write *M* next to the two sentences that are main ideas. Write *S* next to the sentences that give supporting details. Match the *S* sentences to the *M* sentences they support.

1 _____ Jenner took notes and interviewed people who had smallpox.

2 _____ Jenner infected a boy with smallpox.

3 _____ Jenner infected a boy with cowpox.

4 _____ Jenner was a good researcher.

5 _____ Jenner tried a dangerous experiment.

6 _____ Jenner noticed that milkmaids got cowpox, but not smallpox.

**B** Find two details from the text that support each main idea.

| MAIN IDEA | SUPPORTING DETAILS |
|---|---|
| 1 Smallpox was a terrible disease in the eighteenth century. | •<br>•  |
| 2 Jenner made a very important discovery that has helped millions of people. | •<br>•  |

## 7 DISCUSSION

Discuss the following questions in pairs or groups.

1 Do you think Dr. Jenner's experiment with the boy would be possible today? Why or why not?

2 Do you think people are healthier today than they were 250 or 300 years ago? Why or why not?

3 Would you be willing to try a new vaccine or a new medicine? Explain your reasons.

# Saved from Certain Death

## 1 TOPIC PREVIEW

**A** Imagine that you find a cat or a dog that is sick and acting in an unusual way. What would you do? Put a check (✓) next to the best idea. Share your answers with your classmates.

1 _____ try to catch the animal so that you can help it

2 _____ stay away from the animal

3 _____ chase the animal away

4 _____ call the police

5 _____ _____ (your idea)

**B** Read the title of this chapter, look at the picture, and discuss the following questions.

1 What does "certain death" mean?

2 What animal is in the picture? Can it be dangerous? Explain.

3 What do you think the reading is going to be about?

## 2 VOCABULARY PREVIEW

**A** Read the word lists. Put a check (✓) next to the words that you know and can use in a sentence. Compare your answers with a partner. Then look up any unfamiliar words in a dictionary.

| Health Care | Academic Word List | Science |
|---|---|---|
| (in a) **coma** <br> (lose) **consciousness** <br> **diagnose** <br> **symptom** <br> **victim** | **normal** <br> **procedure** <br> **recover** <br> **survive** | **biologist** <br> **stage** (*n.*) <br> (conduct a) **test** |

The chart shows selected words from the reading related to health care, science, and the Academic Word List (AWL). For more information about the AWL, see page 121.

**B** Fill in the blanks with words from Part A.

**1** A person's temperature is not too high or too low. It is _____ .

**2** The doctor conducted a/an _____ to find out what was wrong.

**3** After the accident, the woman did not wake up for three days. She was in a/an _____ .

**4** The player hit his head and lost _____ for a short time.

**5** It took the patient several months to _____ from the illness.

**6** The doctor asked the patient some questions. Then she was able to _____ his illness.

**7** This person studies living things. This person is a/an _____ .

**8** The disease changes as time passes. In the first _____ , the patient gets a fever.

**9** The child had a fever. This was a/an _____ of the illness.

**10** No one understood how he was able to _____ the accident, but he did.

**11** Both doctors followed the same _____ in treating the disease.

**12** The nurse got sick and became one more _____ of the disease.

Preview the questions in Reading Check Part A on page 20. Then read the story.

# Saved from Certain Death

*Jeanna Giese and Dr. Willoughby*

1    Rabies is a terrible disease. The virus usually enters the body through a bite from an animal that has the disease. The bite might not seem serious at first. Then, however, the virus moves to the brain, and the person starts to feel sick. The victim might have hallucinations[1] and other psychological symptoms. In the second stage of the disease, the victim is sometimes afraid of water and cannot drink. Finally, the rabies victim loses consciousness and dies.

2    For thousands of years, rabies meant certain death. Any bite from a strange animal caused great fear. Then, in 1885, a famous French biologist, Louis Pasteur, developed a vaccine. The vaccine stopped the rabies virus. However, it only worked if the victim was given the vaccine at an early stage. In some cases, people did not get the vaccine soon enough. Then rabies symptoms appeared. The vaccine did not work at later stages, and the victim died.

3    Today, people still die from rabies. People often get bites from animals, but they usually do not believe the bite is a serious problem. The bite might not hurt much, so the person doesn't go to the doctor. By the time the person finds out that he or she has rabies, it is too late.

---

[1] *to have hallucinations:* to see or hear things that are not there

The story of Jeanna Giese is a typical example. One Sunday in September of 2005, the 15-year-old girl saw a bat at church. She wanted to help the bat, so she picked it up. The bat bit her finger. It was just a little bite, and Jeanna forgot all about it.

4

About a month later, Jeanna's arm felt strange. She also felt tired and had a headache. Then she began losing consciousness. Her mother took her to the doctor for tests. The symptoms worried the doctors. Then Jeanna's mother remembered the bat bite.

5

The doctors conducted tests to diagnose the problem. The news was not good. Jeanna had rabies. There was nothing they could do. Everything in the medical literature said there was no cure at this stage. Jeanna was going to die.

6

However, one of Jeanna's doctors at the Children's Hospital in Milwaukee, Dr. Rodney Willoughby, did not want to stop trying. He studied rabies and its progress. Rabies is dangerous because it takes over the brain quickly. Dr. Willoughby decided to try an unusual procedure. He wanted to stop the virus from reaching Jeanna's brain, so he put her in a coma. He hoped that by "turning off" her brain for a few days, he could give her immune system enough time to fight the disease.

7

Dogs in the wild can carry rabies.

Jeanna slept while her family and doctors waited in fear. After one week, Jeanna's immune system was fighting the virus on its own. After three more days, Jeanna opened her eyes and recognized her mother. She was alive. Dr. Willoughby's experiment had worked.

8

Jeanna spent two years recovering. She had to learn to talk again and to do many other things. Today, she is like other normal young women. However, there is one difference: Jeanna Giese is the first and only unvaccinated human in history to survive rabies.

9

## 4 READING CHECK

**A** Match the event to the name of the person.

1 _____ This person developed a vaccine for rabies.      **a** Rodney Willoughby

2 _____ This person recovered from rabies.      **b** Louis Pasteur

3 _____ This person found a way to treat rabies.      **c** Jeanna Giese

**B** Circle the letter of the best answer.

1 How do people usually get rabies?
   **a** an animal bite      **b** an insect bite      **c** through the air

2 When was a vaccine for rabies created?
   **a** 1880      **b** 1885      **c** 2005

3 Why do people still die from rabies?
   **a** They don't realize the animal that bit them had rabies.
   **b** There is no vaccine for rabies.
   **c** The rabies vaccine is very difficult to find.

4 Where was Jeanna Giese when the bat bit her?
   **a** asleep in bed      **b** at her church      **c** at school

5 Why didn't doctors give Jeanna the rabies vaccine after they found
   out she had rabies?
   **a** They did not have any rabies vaccine at the hospital.
   **b** The vaccine does not work after the symptoms appear.
   **c** They wanted to try an unusual experiment.

6 Why did the doctor put Jeanna in a coma?
   **a** He didn't want her to hurt herself.
   **b** He wanted to give her body time to fight the virus.
   **c** He thought a coma would keep Jeanna alive while they looked
      for a cure.

7 How long was Jeanna in a coma?
   **a** 3 days      **b** 10 days      **c** 2 years

8 What is Jeanna Giese doing today?
   **a** She is still a patient in a Milwaukee hospital.
   **b** She is helping other people learn about the dangers of rabies.
   **c** She is living a normal life.

# 5 VOCABULARY CHECK

**A** Retell the story. Fill in the blanks with the correct words from the box.

| | | | | |
|---|---|---|---|---|
| biologist | coma | consciousness | diagnosed | normal |
| procedure | stage | survive | symptoms | victim |

In the late nineteenth century, a French _____ , Louis
Pasteur, developed a vaccine for rabies. In the early twenty-first century, an
American teenager needed the vaccine but didn't know it. Jeanna Giese was
just a _____ teenager until she began to feel tired, and she
had a headache. Her mother took her to the doctor to find out why Jeanna
had these _____ . Jeanna's mother remembered a bat bite,
and the doctor _____ the disease. Jeanna was a rabies
_____ .

Dr. Rodney Willoughby knew that Jeanna was in a late
_____ of rabies and there was no cure. He decided to try
an experimental _____ because he wanted to try to save
her life. The doctor put Jeanna in a _____ , and she slept
for ten days. This gave her immune system time to fight the disease. When
Jeanna regained _____ again, the rabies was gone. Jeanna
became the first person to _____ rabies.

**B** Some words often appear together. Circle the words that often appear with the
words in bold. Sometimes, more than one answer is possible.

| | | | | |
|---|---|---|---|---|
| **1** | the doctor | the patient | the hospital | **recovers** |
| **2** | to win | to diagnose | to conduct | **a test** |
| **3** | to lose | to regain | to win | **consciousness** |
| **4** | to fight | to conduct | to survive | **a disease** |
| **5** | a late | an early | the final | **stage** |

## 6 APPLYING READING SKILLS

*Readings often include causes and effects. **Finding causes and effects** will help your understanding of a reading. Sometimes you can find a chain of causes and effects. In other words, one event causes another event that causes another event, and so on.*

**A** Read the list of events. Find the chain of causes and effects. Write the letter of each event in the diagram. The first cause and the last two effects are done for you.

    **a** The person quickly goes to see a doctor.

    **b** The person does not think the bite is serious.

    **c** The person dies.

    **d** An animal with rabies bites a person.

    **e** The person gets a rabies vaccine.

    **f** The person lives.

    **g** The person gets rabies.

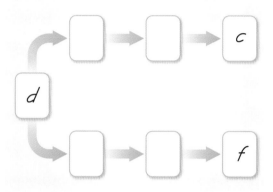

**B** Practice finding causes and effects. Complete this cause and effect chain. Find four events in the story to complete the diagram.

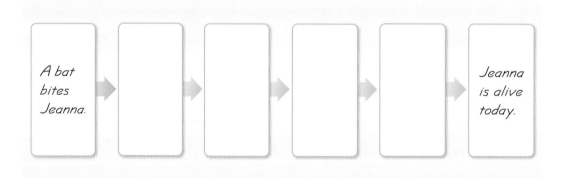

## 7 DISCUSSION

Discuss the following questions in pairs or groups.

    **1** Animals such as dogs and cats can also get rabies. What can people do to protect their pets from rabies?

    **2** Imagine that your neighbor's dog bites you. What would you do?

    **3** Do you know of anyone who survived when he or she was facing "certain death"? Explain.

## VOCABULARY REVIEW

| Chapter **1** | Chapter **2** | Chapter **3** |
|---|---|---|
| **Health Care** | **Health Care** | **Health Care** |
| **fever** · (be in) **pain** · **patient** · **pill** · **prevent** · **treat** (*v.*) | (find a) **cure** · **epidemic** · **immune system** · **infection** · **vaccine** · **virus** | (in a) **coma** · (lose) **consciousness** · **diagnose** · **symptom** · **victim** |
| **Academic Word List** | **Academic Word List** | **Academic Word List** |
| **researcher** · **similar** | **challenge** (*n.*) · **method** · (to test a) **theory** | **normal** · **procedure** · **recover** · **survive** |
| **Business** | **History** | **Science** |
| **company** · **manager** · **on the market** · **produce** (*v.*) | **century** · **era** · (in the) **late** ('20s/'30s/etc.) | **biologist** · **stage** (*n.*) · (conduct a) **test** |

Find words in the chart that match the definitions. Answers to 1–4 are from Chapter 1. Answers to 5–8 are from Chapter 2. Answers to 9–12 are from Chapter 3.

1 To stop something from happening: _____

2 Looking or being almost the same: _____

3 Someone who does a detailed study of a subject: _____

4 An organization that makes or sells things: _____

5 A way of doing something: _____

6 A period of 100 years: _____

7 Something that makes a disease go away: _____

8 The appearance of a disease in a large number of people at the same time: _____

9 A scientist who studies living things: _____

10 To get better after an illness: _____

11 Any feeling or sign of illness that is caused by a disease: _____

12 To name a disease by making an examination: _____

## VOCABULARY IN USE

Work with a partner or small group, and discuss the questions below.

1 If you had a business, what **product** would you sell?

2 How do you **treat** a cold?

3 What can people do to have a strong **immune system**?

4 What health problem do you think is an important **challenge** for doctors?

5 Do you think that flu **vaccines** should be free? Why or why not?

6 What are some reasons people lose **consciousness**?

7 What **procedures** can you use to **prevent infections**?

8 Do you know anyone who **survived** a serious illness or accident?

## ROLE PLAY

Work with a partner. Student A is a newspaper reporter; Student B is one of the people below. Prepare questions. Ask and answer the questions. Then change roles.

- **Felix Hoffmann**

- **Dr. Edward Jenner**

- **Jeanna Giese**

## WRITING

Write a newspaper story about one of the people above. Use notes from the role play or your own ideas. As you write, answer the following questions.

- Who is the person?

- What did the person do?

- When did this take place?

- Why is this person important?

## WEBQUEST

Find more information about the topics in this unit by going on the Internet. Go to www.cambridge.org/readthis and follow the instructions for doing a WebQuest. Search for facts. Have fun. Good luck!

# Animal Studies

## Chapter 4

### Dolphins to the Rescue

Dolphins appear to understand when a person or another animal is in trouble.

**Content areas:**
- Animal Studies
- Behavioral Science

## Chapter 5

### The Gentle Giant from Africa

People lined up along the side of the road in France to watch a giraffe walk by.

**Content areas:**
- Animal Studies
- Physiology

## Chapter 6

### Animal Detectives

Animals can sometimes figure out things that doctors and scientists can't.

**Content areas:**
- Animal Studies
- Health Care

# Dolphins to the Rescue

## 1 TOPIC PREVIEW

**A** Which ocean sports do you think are the most dangerous? Number the following from 1 (the most) to 5 (the least). Share your answers with your classmates.

_____ boating

_____ fishing

_____ scuba diving

_____ surfing

_____ swimming

**B** Read the title of this chapter, look at the picture, and discuss the following questions.

1 Do you practice any of the sports in Part A? Explain.
2 What do you know about dolphins? Have you ever seen a dolphin?
3 What do you think the reading is going to be about?

## 2 VOCABULARY PREVIEW

**A** Read the word lists. Put a check (✓) next to the words that you know and can use in a sentence. Compare your answers with a partner. Then look up any unfamiliar words in a dictionary.

| Animal Studies | Academic Word List | Behavioral Science |
|---|---|---|
| mammal | creative | attract |
| marine | image | behavior |
| shark | institute | control (*v.*) |
| whale | structure | train (*v.*) |

The chart shows selected words from the reading related to animal studies, behavioral science, and the Academic Word List (AWL). For more information about the AWL, see page 121.

**B** Write the word from Part A next to its definition.

**1** Having interesting and unusual ideas: _____

**2** To cause a person or an animal to become interested in someone or something: _____

**3** A picture of what something is like: _____

**4** To teach a person or an animal how to do something: _____

**5** A very large sea animal that breathes air through a hole at the top of its head: _____

**6** The way the parts of an object or a system are organized:

_____

**7** Of or near the sea: _____

**8** Any animal in which the female gives birth to babies, not eggs, and feeds them on milk from her own body: _____

**9** An organization that studies a particular subject: _____

**10** To decide the way something will happen or someone will act:

_____

**11** A particular way of acting: _____

**12** A type of large fish that has sharp teeth: _____

Preview the questions in Reading Check Part A on page 30. Then read the story.

# Dolphins to the Rescue

1 Stories of dolphins saving humans have existed since ancient times. Most of the stories tell of dolphins that saved people from drowning[1] in the ocean. Sailors painted dolphins on their ships, and ancient Greek coins showed a dolphin with a boy riding on its back. Do these images and stories have any truth to them?

2 Todd Endris thinks so. He was sitting on his surfboard off a beach in California waiting for a good wave to ride. Suddenly, a great white shark attacked him. Endris held onto the board, but the shark attacked him a second time. The shark took hold of Endris's leg and tried to pull him into the water. Just then, a group of dolphins arrived. They swam in circles between Endris and the shark. Endris was able to get back on his surfboard and reach the shore. An ambulance rushed him to the hospital. He lost a lot of blood from the attack and almost died. Endris believes the dolphins saved his life.

3 In New Zealand, four lifeguards[2] were in the ocean when a great white shark came near them. It started to swim around them. The

---

[1] *drowning:* dying because you are under water and cannot breathe
[2] *lifeguard:* a person whose job is to watch for the safety of swimmers at pools and beaches

lifeguards thought the shark was going to attack. All of a sudden, a group of dolphins arrived. The dolphins swam between the lifeguards and the shark, and the lifeguards were able to escape.

In the Gulf of Aqaba, a British tourist was swimming. A group of sharks moved in and started to attack him. Three dolphins appeared. They jumped in and out of the water and hit the water with their tails. The sharks swam away. Once again, dolphins saved a human's life. 4

Humans aren't the only ones dolphins rescue. In New Zealand, two whales swam into shallow[3] water. People tried to lead the whales back to deep water, but the whales kept swimming the wrong way. A dolphin appeared and swam between the rescuers and the whales. The whales immediately followed the dolphin as it led them to deep water. 5

Are dolphins as intelligent as they seem? Researchers at the Institute for Marine Mammal Studies in the United States study dolphin behavior. They train dolphins to do various tasks. The dolphins get fish when they complete the tasks. One dolphin is very creative. She caught a seagull.[4] She took it to the trainer, and she got a lot of fish from the trainer. Then the dolphin hid one of the fish and used it later to attract seagulls. She was able to catch another seagull and get more fish. Then she taught this to other dolphins. This type of behavior is clearly a sign of intelligence. 6

How do dolphins know when a human or an animal is in danger? The dolphin's brain structure may help explain this. The dolphin's brain is very heavy. It is 25 percent heavier than a human brain. It is also very large in comparison to the size of the dolphin itself. Humans have three separate areas of the brain, but dolphins have four. In humans, the senses[5] are divided between two areas of the brain. In dolphins, the fourth area controls all the senses. Scientists don't yet understand much about the dolphin brain. Perhaps having all of the senses in one part of the brain means dolphins are more aware of everything around them, including danger to others. 7

Todd Endris doesn't need scientific research. He knows that dolphins are intelligent. Six weeks after the dolphins rescued him, he was back at the beach on his surfboard. Some people probably ask if *he* is intelligent! 8

---

[3] *shallow:* not deep; having only a short distance from the top to the bottom

[4] *seagull:* a large white or gray sea bird

[5] *senses:* the five physical abilities of sight, hearing, smell, taste, and touch

# 4 READING CHECK

**A** Match the place to the event.

1 _____ California

2 _____ New Zealand

3 _____ a research institute

**a** Whales followed dolphins to deeper water.

**b** One dolphin taught other dolphins.

**c** A shark attacked a surfer.

**B** Circle the letter of the best answer.

**1** Since ancient times, people have thought of dolphins as _____ .
   **a** dangerous      **b** rescuers      **c** strange

**2** Todd Endris was _____ when a shark attacked him.
   **a** surfing      **b** fishing      **c** sailing

**3** This reading gives _____ examples of dolphins saving humans.
   **a** one      **b** two      **c** three

**4** How did dolphins save Endris?
   **a** They attacked the shark.
   **b** They swam between Endris and the shark.
   **c** They carried Endris back to shore.

**5** Why did the dolphin at the institute hide the fish?
   **a** because she wanted to eat the fish later
   **b** because the trainer gave her too much fish
   **c** because she wanted to use it to catch a seagull

**6** The dolphin's brain is 25 percent _____ .
   **a** heavier than a person's brain
   **b** larger than other mammals' brains
   **c** of its body weight

**7** In a dolphin's brain, the senses _____ of the brain.
   **a** are in one area
   **b** are divided into three areas
   **c** are divided between two areas

**8** Scientists _____ the dolphin's brain.
   **a** know a lot about
   **b** think that human brains are larger than
   **c** need to do more research on

# 5 VOCABULARY CHECK

**A** Retell the story. Fill in the blanks with the correct words from the box.

| | | | |
|---|---|---|---|
| attract | behavior | controls | creative |
| images | institute | mammals | shark |
| structure | trained | whales | |

In the ancient world, there were many stories and _____
of dolphins rescuing humans. In recent times, dolphins have saved people
from _____ attacks. A dolphin in New Zealand also helped
two _____ swim out of shallow water.

Like humans, dolphins belong to the category of animals called
_____ . Many people think dolphins are intelligent because
of their large brains. Scientists have studied the _____ of
the dolphin brain. One area of the dolphin's brain _____ all
the senses.

Dolphins are _____ , and they can come up with new
ways of doing things. A dolphin in a research _____ in
the United States used fish to _____ seagulls. Then this
dolphin _____ other dolphins to do the same thing. This
_____ certainly appears to show intelligence.

**B** How are each group of words related? Choose the correct category from the box below. Use each category only once.

| | | |
|---|---|---|
| sea animals | places related to water | people |
| actions | words related to water | |

| | | | | |
|---|---|---|---|---|
| 1 _____ | train | control | rescue | attract |
| 2 _____ | tourist | swimmer | lifeguard | trainer |
| 3 _____ | seagull | fish | whale | shark |
| 4 _____ | deep | shallow | marine | wave |
| 5 _____ | sea | ocean | gulf | beach |

## 6 APPLYING READING SKILLS

*Some information that you read is definitely true. It's a fact. Some information is only possibly true. **Reading critically** means asking yourself questions as you read: Is this true? Did this really happen? Am I sure?*

**A** Read the information from the reading in the center of the diagram. Now read sentences 1–4. Write *F* (fact) if the statement is definitely true, according to the excerpt. Write *NS* (not sure) if it is not possible to know if the statement is true.

**1** Dolphins save people from drowning. _____

**2** Sailors paint pictures on their ships. _____

*Stories tell of dolphins that saved people from drowning in the ocean. Sailors painted dolphins on their ships, and ancient Greek coins showed a dolphin with a boy riding on its back.*

**3** Greek coins show a dolphin with a boy on his back. _____

**4** A boy rode on a dolphin's back in ancient Greece. _____

**B** Practice reading critically. If the statements below are facts, write *F* (fact). Write *NS* (not sure) if they are only possibilities or what someone thinks happened.

**1** _____ A shark attacked Todd Endris.

**2** _____ A group of dolphins wanted to rescue Endris.

**3** _____ The dophins swam between Endris and the shark.

**4** _____ The dolphin at the institute used a fish to attract seagulls.

**5** _____ All dolphins are able to train other dolphins.

**6** _____ Dolphins like to save people and other marine mammals.

**7** _____ One area of the dolphin's brain controls all its senses.

**8** _____ Todd Endris is less intelligent than the average dolphin.

## 7 DISCUSSION

Discuss the following questions in pairs or groups.

**1** Which animals do you think are the most intelligent? Why?

**2** Would you eat dolphin meat? Why or why not?

**3** Some people pay a lot of money to swim with dolphins. Is this something you would like to do? Why or why not?

CHAPTER

# 5

# The Gentle Giant from Africa

## 1 TOPIC PREVIEW

**A** Why are the following animals unusual? Share your answers with your classmates.

1 a giraffe

2 an elephant

3 a camel

4 a kangaroo

5 (your idea)

**B** Read the title of this chapter, look at the picture, and discuss the following questions.

1 In which parts of the world do the animals in Part A live in? Explain.

2 The animal in the picture is a giraffe. Why do you think people refer to the giraffe as a "gentle giant"?

3 What do you think the reading is going to be about?

## 2 VOCABULARY PREVIEW

**A** Read the word lists. Put a check (✓) next to the words that you know and can use in a sentence. Compare your answers with a partner. Then look up any unfamiliar words in a dictionary.

| Animal Studies | Academic Word List | Physiology |
| --- | --- | --- |
| creature<br>native (to) (*adj.*)<br>threaten | assist<br>maintain<br>transport | blood pressure<br>dizzy<br>faint (*v.*)<br>muscle<br>pump (*v.*)<br>weigh |

The chart shows selected words from the reading related to animal studies, physiology, and the Academic Word List (AWL). For more information about the AWL, see page 121.

**B** Fill in the blanks with words from Part A.

1 Siamese cats are _____ to Thailand.

2 Our co-workers needed help, so we offered to _____ them.

3 When she stood up quickly, she felt very _____ .

4 This cat is heavy! How much does it _____ ?

5 As people get older, they sometimes get high _____ .

6 The soldiers didn't hurt or _____ anyone from the village.

7 What kind of _____ is that? Is it a wild pig?

8 Are you sick? Please sit down before you _____ .

9 To save gas, try to _____ the same driving speed.

10 Our hearts _____ blood through our bodies.

11 It is less expensive to _____ food by truck or train than by airplane.

12 He hurt a/an _____ in his back when he was lifting something.

Preview the questions in Reading Check Part A on page 37. Then read the story.

# The Gentle Giant from Africa

All over the world, people find giraffes amazing. The giraffe is
the tallest animal in the world. Its legs and tail are taller than most
people. Its tongue is very long, 18 inches. The front part of its tongue
is an unusual color, black. Unlike most other large animals, giraffes do
not threaten people. Yet, to many scientists, the most amazing thing
about this gentle giant is something that we cannot see – its heart.

To understand how amazing the giraffe's heart is, put your head
lower than your heart. Keep it there for a few minutes. Then, lift your
head up very quickly. Do you feel dizzy? This is the effect of a change
in blood pressure. The heart has to quickly pump blood to your brain
to stop you from feeling dizzy or from fainting.

When a giraffe lifts its head up from the ground, it has to lift its
550-pound neck (249 kilograms) more than 15 feet (4.6 meters) in
the air. How can it do this without fainting? The giraffe's heart is
extremely large. It is almost two feet (0.6 meter) long and weighs about
24 pounds (10.9 kilograms). It can pump 16 gallons (60.5 liters) of blood
in a minute. The large artery[1] that carries blood from the heart up the

1

2

3

---

[1] *artery:* one of the thick tubes that carry blood from the heart to other parts of
the body

long neck of the giraffe is also unusual because it has a muscle in it. This muscle assists in maintaining the giraffe's blood pressure.

4     In 1988, a writer, Michael Allin, read a short note in a magazine about the first giraffe to come to France. He knew that giraffes were native only to Africa. So he wanted to know more about this giraffe: Where did it come from, and why? He spent ten years trying to find out, and then he wrote a book about it.

5     Allin learned that the giraffe arrived in Marseille, a city in the south of France, in 1826. It was a gift to the king of France, Charles X. Then Allin went to Ethiopia, in East Africa, where the giraffe was born. He traveled to Egypt on the Nile River. This was the same way the giraffe came to Egypt. In Egypt, he discovered the reason for the gift. Muhammad Ali, an important Egyptian leader, did not want the French to enter a war. He decided that a very special gift would help, so he sent the giraffe to King Charles X.

6     It was difficult to transport a giraffe in 1826. It traveled from Egypt to France on a ship. The giraffe was so tall that it couldn't fit in the lower deck[2] of the ship. This was quite a problem until someone decided to cut a hole in the top deck of the ship. The giraffe's legs were below, and its long neck came up through the hole.

7     No one knew how to get such a large animal from Marseille to Paris. Therefore, the giraffe had to walk the 550 miles (885 kilometers). All along the way, people came to watch the gentle giant walk past. Six weeks after it left Marseille, the giraffe finally arrived in Paris, where 100,000 people came to see this amazing creature. Today, we still look at the giraffe in amazement. There is no other animal like it on earth.

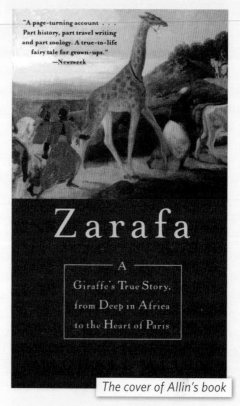

The cover of Allin's book

---

[2] *deck:* the floor on a ship

# 4 READING CHECK

**A** Are these statements true or false? Write *T* (true) or *F* (false).

1 _____ A giraffe's heart pumps blood to its head quickly.

2 _____ Michael Allin wanted to learn about the first giraffe
that came to France.

3 _____ In the early 1800s, giraffes were common in Europe.

**B** Circle the letter of the best answer.

1 Giraffes are called "gentle" because they are _____ .
   **a** big-hearted      **b** taller than people      **c** not threatening

2 The most amazing thing about a giraffe is its _____ .
   **a** tongue      **b** heart      **c** feet

3 How much weight does a giraffe have to lift when it raises its head?
   **a** 15 pounds      **b** 24 pounds      **c** 550 pounds

4 What is unusual about the artery in a giraffe's neck?
   **a** It has a muscle in it.
   **b** It weighs 24 pounds.
   **c** It also carries blood to the legs.

5 Why did Michael Allin go to Africa?
   **a** He loved giraffes from the time he was a boy.
   **b** He was interested in the story of Muhammad Ali.
   **c** He wanted to travel the way the first giraffe came to France.

6 Muhammad Ali gave the giraffe to _____ .
   **a** the king of France
   **b** the French people
   **c** the Egyptian leader

7 What did they have to do to transport the giraffe by ship?
   **a** cut a hole in the deck
   **b** add a taller deck to the ship
   **c** build a new ship

8 Why did the giraffe walk to Paris?
   **a** It was the only way to get there.
   **b** People wanted to see the giraffe.
   **c** It was too big to go in an airplane.

## 5 VOCABULARY CHECK

**A** Retell the story. Fill in the blanks with the correct words from the box.

| | | |
|---|---|---|
| blood pressure | creature | dizzy |
| faint | maintain | muscle |
| native | pump | transport |

The giraffe is _____ to Africa. In 1826, an Egyptian
<br>1
ruler sent a giraffe to King Charles X of France. It was very difficult to

_____ a giraffe in those days, so it had to walk from the
<br>2
coast of France all the way to Paris. People came out to see the giant animal

walk by.

Even today, scientists think the giraffe is an amazing

_____ . The giraffe's heart has to be large in order to
<br>3
_____ blood to its brain. The giraffe's main artery in its
<br>4
neck is unusual because it has a _____ in it. This helps
<br>5
to keep the giraffe's _____ normal. It is important for the
<br>6
giraffe to _____ normal blood pressure. Without it, the
<br>7
giraffe would feel _____ . It might _____
<br>8 9
and fall to the ground.

**B** Fill in the blanks with the correct form of the word.

| Verb | Noun |
|---|---|
| assist | assistance |
| threaten | threat |
| weigh | weight |

**1** How much does a giraffe _____ ?

**2** Few animals _____ giraffes because they are so large.

**3** The salesperson said, "How may I _____ you?"

**4** I eat healthy food, so I am not worried about my _____ .

**5** High blood pressure increases the _____ of heart disease.

**6** She is 90 years old, but she lives by herself and doesn't need any

_____ .

## 6 APPLYING READING SKILLS

*Using reference materials*, such as atlases, encyclopedias, and Web sites, after you read is sometimes necessary to get the most complete understanding of a reading.

**A** Look at this map of northern Africa and southern Europe. Find the following places that are mentioned in the reading. Put each number in the correct place on the map.

1 Ethiopia

2 Paris

3 The Nile River

4 France

5 Marseille

6 Egypt

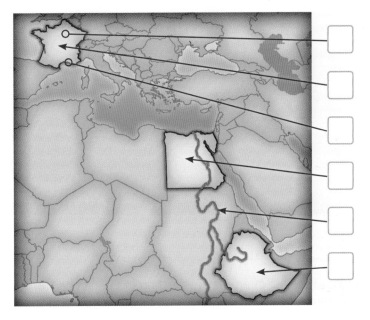

**B** On the map in Part A, draw a line that shows the way that the giraffe probably traveled from Ethiopia to Paris. Use a colored pen or pencil.

## 7 DISCUSSION

Discuss the following questions in pairs or groups.

1 Do you think that the giraffe was a good gift? Why or why not?

2 Some people dream about going to Africa to see many different animals in the wild. Is this something you would like to do? Why or why not?

3 Sometimes people take animals from the wild and put them in zoos and circuses. Sometimes people kill wild animals for sport or so they can sell parts of the animal for money. Do you think people should do these things? Why or why not?

# Animal Detectives

## 1 TOPIC PREVIEW

**A** Read the list of animals. Which animals can be trained to perform jobs for humans? Put a check (✓) next to your choices. Share your answers with your classmates.

1 _____ dogs

2 _____ cats

3 _____ horses

4 _____ birds

5 _____ _____ (your idea)

**B** Read the title of this chapter, look at the picture, and discuss the following questions.

1  What are the people and animals in the picture doing? Is this typical or unusual in your culture?

2  Do you or your family have pets? If so, what kind?

3  What do you think the reading is going to be about?

# 2 VOCABULARY PREVIEW

**A** Read the word lists. Put a check (✓) next to the words that you know and can use in a sentence. Compare your answers with a partner. Then look up any unfamiliar words in a dictionary.

| Animal Studies | Academic Word List | Health Care |
|---|---|---|
| sniff<br>species | accurately<br>detect<br>identify<br>predict<br>site | cancer<br>deadly<br>lab test<br>nursing home<br>sample (*n.*) |

The chart shows selected words from the reading related to animal studies, health care, and the Academic Word List (AWL). For more information about the AWL, see page 121.

**B** Fill in the blanks with words from Part A.

**1** The doctor wanted more information and sent the patient to have another _____ .

**2** Doctors can now _____ very small amounts of dangerous chemicals in the body.

**3** Smell is very important to dogs. They _____ everything.

**4** The nurse made a mistake and did not measure the medicine _____ .

**5** _____ is a disease that affects millions of people.

**6** When the elderly man got out of the hospital, he had to go to a/an _____ because he still needed special care.

**7** The _____ of the new museum is in an old, historic part of the city.

**8** Modern medicine has helped people recover from diseases that used to be _____ .

**9** Scientists study many different _____ of animals.

**10** The doctor took a/an _____ of blood and sent it for testing.

**11** The professor asked us to _____ several types of whales.

**12** No one can _____ the future.

Preview the questions in Reading Check Part A on page 44. Then read the story.

# Animal Detectives

Oscar the cat

1    Millions of people have dogs and cats as pets. Dogs also help some
people who need assistance in daily living. Dogs guide the blind[1] and
act as ears for the deaf. Now, recent stories in the news say that dogs
and cats can also help doctors.

2    Oscar the cat lives in a nursing home, where people stay when they
need special care when they are very ill or at the end of their lives.
Cats, small dogs, and birds are often kept as pets in nursing homes.
They entertain people and provide friendship. However, Oscar is
different from the normal nursing home pet.

3    Every day, Oscar walks in and out of the patients' rooms. The
nurses say that he "does the rounds"[2] just like a doctor. He looks at
each patient and sniffs. Then he usually leaves the room. However,
when Oscar decides to stay and gets on the bed next to the patient,
the nurses call the doctor and the patient's family. According to the
nurses, Oscar has accurately predicted the death of 25 patients so far.

---

[1] *the blind:* people who are not able to see
[2] *do the rounds:* visit all the patients regularly

Oscar's story is just that – a story. No one has done research to find out how accurate Oscar the cat really is. There may be a different reason Oscar stays in the rooms of people who are going to die. However, two research studies have found other examples of animals that help doctors. These studies found that some dogs can detect cancer.

In the first study, cancer patients breathed into tubes.[3] Scientists then trained five dogs to sit or lie down when they smelled the breath samples with cancer. Next came the real test. The dogs smelled more than 150 different breath samples from both healthy patients and patients with cancer. One dog was 97 percent accurate in identifying the 86 samples of people with cancer. Even the dog with the lowest score identified 88 percent of the cancer samples.

In the second study, several dogs identified a sample that the researchers thought was cancer-free. The researchers sent it back for more lab tests. This time, the tests showed that the sample actually did show signs of cancer. The dogs identified cancer that the first tests missed!

These research results do not surprise many pet owners. A dog named Trudi kept sniffing at her owner's leg. The owner went to the doctor, who found that the man had melanoma. This is a form of skin cancer that can be deadly. The dog identified it early, before it spread.[4] Another patient was treated for cancer, but her dog kept sniffing and making noises at the cancer site. The doctor had not removed all the cancer. Once again, a dog identified its owner's cancer.

What makes dogs a species of animal that is so good at detecting cancer? Diseases such as cancer produce smells. Dogs can smell as much as 10,000 times better than people, and much more of the dog's brain is related to the sense of smell. Smelling things is a large part of a dog's life.

Will a visit to the doctor soon include a sniff from a friendly animal? Some people think this is not a bad idea. It is less expensive than a lab test, and it doesn't hurt! Pet owners: Pay attention when your dog or cat starts acting differently.

---

[3] *tube:* a small, narrow container that scientists use

[4] *spread:* moved to another place

## 4 READING CHECK

**A** Circle the letter of the best answer.

1 What does Oscar the cat seem to know?
   **a** who has a disease    **b** who likes cats    **c** who is about to die

2 What can the dogs in the story detect?
   **a** cancer    **b** patients    **c** medicine

3 What sense helps the dogs do this?
   **a** their eyesight    **b** their sense of smell    **c** their hearing

**B** Are these statements true or false? Write *T* (true) or *F* (false). Then correct any false statements.

1 _____ Oscar the cat stays with patients who are about to die.

_____

2 _____ Oscar is part of a research study.

_____

3 _____ Oscar smells each patient in the nursing home every day.

_____

4 _____ In the first study, dogs sniffed 150 breath samples from patients with cancer.

_____

5 _____ In a research study, dogs found cancer that earlier tests missed.

_____

6 _____ Some pet dogs have helped detect cancer in their owners.

_____

7 _____ Dogs are good at detecting cancer because they see very well.

_____

8 _____ The reading discusses three research studies.

_____

## 5 VOCABULARY CHECK

**A** Retell the story. Fill in the blanks with the correct words from the box.

| | | | |
|---|---|---|---|
| accurately | deadly | detect | lab test |
| nursing home | predict | samples | site |
| sniff | species | | |

Oscar is a pet cat in a/an _____ 1 . Amazingly, he seems to be able to _____ 2 when patients are going to die. Cats are not the only _____ 3 of animal with special abilities to assist in the health-care field. Some dogs are able to _____ 4 cancer. Researchers took breath _____ 5 from both healthy and sick people. Then they had dogs _____ 6 the tubes. In one test, the dogs _____ 7 identified cancer between 88 and 97 percent of the time. In another test, dogs identified cancer that a/an _____ 8 had missed. One dog owner had an operation to remove skin cancer. After the operation, the dog kept smelling the _____ 9 of the operation. Doctors had not removed all the cancer. This could have been a/an _____ 10 mistake.

**B** Unscramble the words to complete the sentences.

**1** The lab worker did not enter the data _____ . (ltyeaucrac)

**2** Lab tests help doctors to _____ diseases. (fiitdyen)

**3** Until recently, _____ was a deadly disease, but now there are treatments. (recnac)

**4** Dogs and cats are different _____ . (ecsipes)

**5** She needed more assistance, so she went to a/an _____ when she left the hospital. (hisnenougmr) (two words)

## 6 APPLYING READING SKILLS

*Your reading speed is the number of words you can read per minute.*
***Increasing your reading speed*** *will make it easier to do all the reading for your classes. Timing yourself when you read will help you read faster.*

**A** Reread "Animal Detectives" on page 42, and time yourself. Write your starting time, your finishing time, and the number of minutes it took you to read. Then calculate your reading speed.

> **Story title:** "Animal Detectives" (554 words)
> Starting time: _____
> Finishing time: _____
> Total reading time: _____ minutes
> *Reading speed: _____ words per minute

*To calculate your reading speed, divide the number of words in the text (554) by your total reading time (the number of minutes you needed to read the text).

**B** Now reread either "Dolphins to the Rescue" (592 words) on page 28 or "The Gentle Giant from Africa" (538 words) on page 35. Time yourself. Write the title of the story and your times below. Then calculate your reading speed.

> **Story title:** _____ ( _____ words)
> Starting time: _____
> Finishing time: _____
> Total reading time: _____ minutes
> Reading speed: _____ words per minute

## 7 DISCUSSION

Discuss the following questions in pairs or groups.

1 Does anything in the reading "Animal Detectives" surprise you? If so, what and why?

2 What do you think is the explanation for Oscar's behavior?

3 Would you like to work with animals in some way? As an animal trainer, an animal doctor (veterinarian), a researcher, or some other way? Why or why not?

## VOCABULARY REVIEW

| Chapter **4** | Chapter **5** | Chapter **6** |
|---|---|---|
| **Animal Studies** | **Animal Studies** | **Animal Studies** |
| mammal · marine · shark · whale | creature · native (to) (*adj.*) · threaten | sniff · species |
| **Academic Word List** | **Academic Word List** | **Academic Word List** |
| creative · image · institute · structure | assist · maintain · transport | accurately · detect · identify · predict · site |
| **Behavioral Science** | **Physiology** | **Health Care** |
| attract · behavior · control (*v.*) · train (*v.*) | blood pressure · dizzy · faint (*v.*) · muscle · pump (*v.*) · weigh | cancer · deadly · lab test · nursing home · sample (*n.*) |

Find words in the chart that match the definitions. Answers to 1–4 are from Chapter 4. Answers to 5–8 are from Chapter 5. Answers to 9–12 are from Chapter 6.

**1** A picture of what something is like: _____

**2** Any animal in which the female gives birth to babies, not eggs, and feeds them on milk from her own body: _____

**3** To teach a person or an animal how to do something: _____

**4** Having interesting and unusual ideas: _____

**5** To take action to help someone or support something: _____

**6** Describing someone who was born in a place: _____

**7** To find out how heavy something is: _____

**8** Any living thing, especially an animal: _____

**9** A place where elderly people live and receive care when they can no longer care for themselves: _____

**10** To smell something by taking in air through the nose: _____

**11** Doing something correctly, without making a mistake: _____

**12** A disease in which cells in the body grow without control: _____

## VOCABULARY IN USE

Work with a partner or small group, and discuss the questions below.

1 What are some animal **species** that we need to protect? Explain.

2 What **marine mammal** do you find most interesting? Why?

3 In what ways is the **behavior** of dogs different from cats?

4 Has an animal ever **threatened** you or someone you know? What happened?

5 How do you think people **transport** giraffes or other large animals today?

6 What are some **creatures** that have **deadly** bites?

7 **Identify** one important thing that you would like to do in the next year. Explain.

8 What do you **predict** your life will be like in five years?

## ROLE PLAY

Work with a partner. Student A is an animal expert and trainer who works with one of the creatures in the readings (a dolphin, a giraffe, a dog, or a cat). Student B is a visitor. The expert tells the visitor about training the dolphin, giraffe, dog, or cat. The visitor asks questions about the animal and its special characteristics. Then change roles. This time, the expert chooses a different animal.

## WRITING

Write a first-person story about one of the situations below. Answer these questions: What do you see? How do you feel? What happens?

- Imagine that dolphins saved you from a shark attack.

- Imagine that you are traveling with the first giraffe to Paris.

- Imagine that you are a doctor in the nursing home where Oscar the cat lives.

## WEBQUEST

Find more information about the topics in this unit by going on the Internet. Go to www.cambridge.org/readthis and follow the instructions for doing a WebQuest. Search for facts. Have fun. Good luck!

# UNIT

# 3

# Food and Nutrition

## Chapter 7

### How the Kiwi Got Its Name

An ugly little fruit journeyed around the world before it got its new name.

**Content areas:**
- Food and Nutrition
- Agriculture

## Chapter 8

### The Fifth Taste

A French chef and a Japanese food chemist discovered the fifth taste, but no one believed them.

**Content areas:**
- Food and Nutrition
- Culinary Arts

## Chapter 9

### Eat Less, Live Longer?

You may be suprised by what scientists say could be the secret to a longer and healthier life.

**Content areas:**
- Food and Nutrition
- Biology

# How the Kiwi Got Its Name

## 1 TOPIC PREVIEW

**A** Which fruits do you eat the most? Number the fruits from 1 (the most) to 5 (the least). Share your answers with your classmates.

_____ orange

_____ banana

_____ apple

_____ melon

_____ _____ (your idea)

**B** Read the title of this chapter, look at the picture, and discuss the following questions.

**1** Which fruits in the picture do you eat? Do you know their names in English?

**2** How do you eat fruit? Do you eat it as dessert? As a snack? In a salad? Do you cook with fruit? Explain.

**3** What do you think the reading is going to be about?

# 2 VOCABULARY PREVIEW

**A** Read the word lists. Put a check (✓) next to the words that you know and can use in a sentence. Compare your answers with a partner. Then look up any unfamiliar words in a dictionary.

| Food and Nutrition | Academic Word List | Agriculture |
|---|---|---|
| mineral<br>nutritious<br>vitamin | expand<br>source<br>symbol | crop<br>grow<br>harvest (*v.*)<br>import tax<br>plant (*v.*)<br>seed |

The chart shows selected words from the reading related to food and nutrition, agriculture, and the Academic Word List (AWL). For more information about the AWL, see page 121.

**B** Fill in the blanks with words from Part A.

1 Fruits and vegetables need water to _____ .

2 The _____ for the U.S. dollar is "$."

3 Be careful when you eat this orange! One of the pieces may still have a/an _____ in it.

4 It is important to eat _____ food.

5 Farmers usually _____ in the spring.

6 The new _____ of corn will be ready in a few days.

7 Some people think _____ C prevents colds.

8 In the fall, apple growers _____ their apples.

9 Sugar producers asked the government to put a/an _____ on sugar from other countries.

10 Bananas are a good _____ of potassium.

11 Iron is an important _____ that your body needs to stay healthy.

12 They bought more land so that they could _____ their farm.

**3** READING

Preview the questions in Reading Check Part A on page 54. Then read the story.

# How the Kiwi Got Its Name

1     It is one of the ugliest little fruits in the world. Many people don't know how to eat it and have never tried it. This fruit, however, is a multi-billion-dollar super food, a food that is very nutritious.

2     This fruit's skin is brown and looks like the fur of a monkey. This explains one of the fruit's original names, which means "monkey peach" in Chinese. The Chinese first grew it in the Chang Kiang Valley about 700 years ago. It became a favorite food of the rulers. They liked the bright green color on the inside of the fruit and its sweet taste.

3     When people from other parts of the world began traveling in China, they discovered this unusual-looking fruit. In 1904, a woman from New Zealand, Isabel Fraser, traveled to China. There, she ate a monkey peach. She liked its taste, so she took some seeds back with her to New Zealand. She gave the seeds to Thomas Allison. Thomas and his brother, Alexander, owned an orchard.[1] Alexander Allison planted Fraser's seeds and harvested the first fruit in 1910.

---

[1] *orchard:* land where farmers plant fruit trees

The climate of New Zealand was perfect for the monkey peach, and soon the fruit became popular there. However, New Zealanders had trouble pronouncing the name in Chinese. They decided to call it a "Chinese gooseberry"[2] because the fruit is green, like a gooseberry.

By the 1950s, New Zealand had more Chinese gooseberries than they could eat. Fruit growers wanted to expand their markets to other countries. However, they had a problem. Some countries had an import tax on berries. To avoid the tax, the growers decided to change the name. The fruit looked like a tiny melon, so they decided to call it *melonette*.[3] This name seemed like a good idea until they learned that there was also a high tax on melons. What could they call it?

The fruit growers got together to discuss a new name. Someone suggested the name *kiwi*. The furry kiwi bird is a symbol of New Zealand, and New Zealanders are sometimes called Kiwis. The growers all agreed, and this small green Chinese fruit took the name of a symbol of New Zealand.

When the kiwi fruit first appeared in other countries, most people thought it was strange. They didn't know how to eat it, and they didn't like the rough skin. Eventually, people learned to remove the furry skin and eat the sweet inside part. They started to enjoy it.

Recently, food scientists have discovered some surprising information about the kiwi. One small kiwi fruit has more vitamin C than any other fruit. It is also a great source of fiber and provides the body with important minerals, such as calcium and potassium.

Today the kiwi is more popular than ever. It is a major crop in many countries, including Chile and Italy. In New Zealand, it is the number one export. Farmers there even export this healthy and delicious food to China, where it all began.

---

[2] *gooseberry:* a type of berry; other examples of berries are strawberries, blueberries, and raspberries

[3] *melonette:* the French word for "little melon"

# 4 READING CHECK

**A** The kiwi fruit had different names over time. Write *1*, *2*, and *3* next to the first, second, and third names it had.

**a** _____ melonette

**b** _____ monkey peach

**c** _____ Chinese gooseberry

**B** Are these statements true or false? Write *T* (true) or *F* (false). Then correct any false statements.

**1** _____ The kiwi fruit was from New Zealand originally.

_____

**2** _____ The skin of the kiwi is not like the skin of other fruit.

_____

**3** _____ Isabel Fraser planted the first kiwi seeds in New Zealand.

_____

**4** _____ On the inside, the kiwi is the same color as a gooseberry.

_____

**5** _____ Growers changed the name of the fruit to "Chinese gooseberry" because of import taxes in other countries.

_____

**6** _____ A "kiwi" may be a person, a bird, or a fruit.

_____

**7** _____ The kiwi fruit was immediately successful in other countries.

_____

**8** _____ The kiwi is nutritious because it has vitamins, minerals, and fiber.

_____

## 5 VOCABULARY CHECK

**A** Retell the story. Fill in the blanks with the correct words from the box.

| | | | |
|---|---|---|---|
| crop | expand | grew | harvested |
| import taxes | minerals | nutritious | plant |
| seeds | source | symbol | vitamins |

In 1904, a woman from New Zealand, Isabel Fraser, traveled to China. There, she tasted a little brown fruit. The Chinese called it the "monkey peach." Fraser liked its taste, so she brought the first monkey peach _____ from China to New Zealand. She gave them to Thomas and Alexander Allison to _____ in their orchard. In 1910, the Allison brothers _____ their first _____ of fruit. The fruit _____ well in New Zealand, where it was called the "Chinese gooseberry."

By the 1950s New Zealand had more Chinese gooseberries than they could eat. Growers wanted to _____ their markets to other countries. However, many countries had _____ on berries, so the search for a new name began. The growers thought about "melonette," but there was a high tax in some countries on melons. They finally decided on *kiwi*, the name of the furry bird that is a/an _____ of New Zealand. Today many countries grow the kiwi fruit. It is a popular fruit all over the world.

**B** Use words from the box in Part A to complete this advertisement.

Nutri-Delicious is an amazing new food. Add it to anything you eat for a wonderfully _____ health aid. Nutri-Delicious is full of _____ from A to Z and _____ like iron and calcium. It's also an excellent _____ of fiber. Don't wait. Buy Nutri-Delicious today!

## 6 APPLYING READING SKILLS

> ***Asking and answering "Why?" questions*** *about information in a reading can help you develop critical thinking and reading skills.*

**A** Look back at the reading to find the answers to these "Why?" questions.

Why did the Chinese call the kiwi fruit "monkey peach"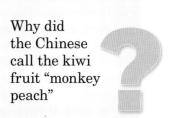

Why did Isabel Fraser take the monkey peach seeds back to New Zealand

Why is the kiwi popular today

**B** Practice using "Why?" questions. Write two or more "Why?" questions about the reading. Then ask and answer the questions with a partner.

1 Why _____

_____?

2 Why _____

_____?

## 7 DISCUSSION

Discuss the following questions in pairs or groups.

1 Are there foods that you like now that you didn't like when you were younger? Are there foods that you don't like now that you liked when you were younger? Explain.

2 What are some foods that grow in your area? What are some foods that are imported? Where do the imported foods come from?

3 What foods have recently become popular where you live? Have you tried them?

# CHAPTER
# 8
# The Fifth Taste

## 1 TOPIC PREVIEW

**A** What foods are your favorites? Make a list of the five foods that you enjoy most. Share your answers with your classmates.

1 _____

2 _____

3 _____

4 _____

5 _____

**B** Read the title of this chapter, look at the picture, and discuss the following questions.

1 Describe the taste of each of your favorite foods. Is it sweet, sour, bitter, or salty?

2 Describe the taste of each food in the photograph.

3 What do you think the reading is going to be about?

## 2 VOCABULARY PREVIEW

**A** Read the word lists. Put a check (✓) next to the words that you know and can use in a sentence. Compare your answers with a partner. Then look up any unfamiliar words in a dictionary.

| Food and Nutrition | Academic Word List | Culinary Arts |
|---|---|---|
| additive<br>food chemist<br>seaweed | isolate<br>occur<br>physical<br>respond (to) | chef<br>flavor (v.)<br>fry<br>ingredient<br>sauce |

The chart shows selected words from the reading related to food and nutrition, culinary arts, and the Academic Word List (AWL). For more information about the AWL, see page 121.

**B** Fill in the blanks with words from Part A.

1 She cooks in a large restaurant. She is an excellent _____ .

2 You need an egg to make this cake. The egg is an important

  _____ .

3 He studies and does experiments with food. He is a/an _____ .

4 Scientists had to _____ the virus so that they could make a vaccine.

5 She felt better as soon as her body began to _____ to the medicine.

6 She poured the thick _____ on top of the meat.

7 Herbs, salt, and pepper give food more taste. They _____ food.

8 He had a bad _____ reaction to the food.

9 "How are you going to cook the chicken?"  "I'm going to
  _____ it."

10 Sometimes answers to problems _____ to us when we aren't trying to think about them.

11 The food contained a/an _____ to help it stay fresh.

12 The ocean contains a lot of _____ . As a food, this is a great source of minerals for the human body.

Preview the question in Reading Check Part A on page 61. Then read the story.

# The Fifth Taste

1　　Since ancient times, people have recognized four basic tastes. One is sour, like a lemon. Another is salty, like potato chips. The third is sweet, like sugar. The fourth taste is bitter, like coffee or unsweetened chocolate.

2　　It wasn't until the late 1800s in Paris that a famous chef, Auguste Escoffier, made a new discovery about taste. First, he fried beef in a pan at a very high heat until it was brown. Then he added a liquid and scraped the browned meat from the bottom of the pan. The taste of the browned meat stock[1] wasn't sweet, salty, bitter, or sour. Escoffier was a chef, not a scientist, but he was sure he had found a fifth taste. He used his discovery to create some of his famous sauces.

3　　About 20 years later in Japan, Kikunae Ikeda was eating a bowl of soup. As he ate, he tried to decide what made the soup so delicious. His wife told him how she made it. The basic ingredient was *dashi*, a stock made with kelp, or dried seaweed. Suddenly, it occurred to him, too: there weren't four tastes. There was a fifth taste, and this was it – the deep, full taste in the stock!

4　　Ikeda was a food chemist. He decided to use his knowledge and skills as a chemist. He wanted to know exactly what this fifth taste was. He went to work in his laboratory and found the answer –

---

[1] *stock:* a liquid used to add flavor to food that is made by boiling meat or fish bones or vegetables in water

glutamate. Glutamate is an amino acid[2] that is produced when living things begin to die. For example, the production of glutamate happens when cheese ages or meat cooks. Its taste is very different from the other four tastes. Ikeda decided to call the taste *umami*. This comes from a Japanese word that means "delicious."

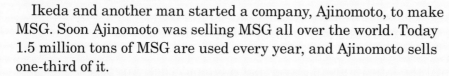

*Kikunae Ikeda*

5    Ikeda continued to work with glutamate. He wanted to use this natural amino acid to make food more delicious. He was looking for a way to make umami similar to salt or sugar – an additive to flavor food. Finally, he isolated the glutamate and found that he could add salt (sodium) to it. Monosodium glutamate, or MSG, was the food additive he was looking for. It produced the fifth taste.

6    Ikeda and another man started a company, Ajinomoto, to make MSG. Soon Ajinomoto was selling MSG all over the world. Today 1.5 million tons of MSG are used every year, and Ajinomoto sells one-third of it.

7    Ikeda's MSG was a huge commercial success, but some scientists did not believe umami was really a fifth taste. They continued to believe that there were only four tastes. Then, in 2000, almost 100 years after Ikeda's discovery, scientists found physical proof. The human tongue contains tiny receptors, or taste buds,[3] which allow us to tell the difference between tastes. Scientists found that these receptors responded to glutamate in a special way. In fact, they found that the receptors responded in that way only to glutamate, and not to any of the other four tastes.

8    It turns out that the great French chef Escoffier was right. There are five tastes, not just four. Today, chefs in many parts of the world are using their knowledge of this fifth taste to create a new type of cuisine. The chefs are trying to use less salt and less butter. They are using foods with a lot of natural glutamate. The result is healthy food that is also very tasty. It's delicious. It's umami!

---

[2] *amino acid:* a chemical substance found in plants and animals

[3] *taste buds:* groups of cells on the tongue that allow people to recognize tastes

# 4 READING CHECK

**A** Circle the number of the sentence that best expresses the main idea of the reading.

1 A chef and a chemist identified the fifth taste.
2 Amino acids are in the foods we eat.
3 People all over the world use MSG to flavor food.

**B** Circle the letter of the best answer.

1 Escoffier was famous for his _____ .
   **a** sauces   **b** fifth taste   **c** umami

2 Ikeda was eating _____ when he discovered the fifth taste.
   **a** seaweed   **b** soup   **c** sauce

3 Which of these is *not* true?
   **a** Glutamate is the fifth taste.
   **b** Glutamate is an amino acid.
   **c** Glutamate is only in cooked food.

4 Escoffier's sauces had the fifth taste because _____ .
   **a** they were very famous
   **b** he made a sauce with seaweed stock
   **c** he cooked the meat at a high temperature

5 In his laboratory, Ikeda added _____ to glutamate.
   **a** sugar
   **b** a stock
   **c** sodium

6 People add MSG to food because it makes food _____ .
   **a** healthier
   **b** taste better
   **c** cook more quickly

7 For many years, scientists did not believe Ikeda because _____ .
   **a** they did not like the taste of MSG
   **b** the amino acid glutamate did not exist
   **c** there was no physical proof of a fifth taste

8 Special receptors on the _____ respond to glutamate.
   **a** heart
   **b** tongue
   **c** nose

## 5 VOCABULARY CHECK

**A** Retell the story. Fill in the blanks with the correct words from the box.

| | | | |
|---|---|---|---|
| additive | chef | flavor | food chemist |
| fried | ingredients | isolate | occurred |
| physical | respond | sauces | seaweed |

Escoffier, a famous French _____ , discovered a

fifth taste when he _____ meat at a very high heat
<sub>2</sub>

until it was brown. This was the way he made stock to use in his

famous _____ .
<sub>3</sub>

A Japanese _____ named Kikunae Ikeda was
<sub>4</sub>

eating a delicious soup that his wife had made. One of the main

_____ of the stock was dried _____ .
<sub>5</sub>                                                          <sub>6</sub>

As he ate, it _____ to him that the soup had a fifth
<sub>7</sub>

taste. Ikeda did experiments in his laboratory. He found that the taste

came from glutamate. He was able to _____ glutamate
<sub>8</sub>

and add sodium to it. He created a/an _____ called
<sub>9</sub>

MSG that people use to _____ food.
<sub>10</sub>

Almost 100 years later, scientists found _____ proof
<sub>11</sub>

that both Escoffier and Ikeda were right. The tongue has receptors that

_____ only to this fifth taste.
<sub>12</sub>

**B** Which preposition follows the words in bold? Circle the answer.

**1** She didn't **respond** (in / from / to) the question.

**2** The answer **occurred** (in / from / to) her later.

**3** MSG is an **additive** (in / from / to) many foods.

**4** Sugar is an **ingredient** (in / from / to) most sodas.

**5** The doctor **isolated** the sick patients (out / from / to) the healthy ones.

## 6 APPLYING READING SKILLS

*Sometimes you are not sure about the meaning of a word or phrase in a reading. **Finding examples and definitions** of the word or phrase can help make its meaning clearer.*

**A** Draw a line from the words on the left to an example or a definition from the reading on the right.

| WORDS | EXAMPLES AND DEFINITIONS |
|---|---|
| salty | things found on the tongue that can tell different tastes |
| umami | like the taste of sugar |
| taste buds | like the taste of potato chips |
| kelp | an abbreviation for "monosodium glutamate" |
| sweet | related to the Japanese word for "delicious" |
| MSG | another word for "dried seaweed" |

**B** Practice finding examples and definitions. Look back at the reading. Find examples or definitions of the following words.

| WORDS | EXAMPLES AND DEFINITIONS |
|---|---|
| sodium | _____ |
| bitter | _____ |
| fried | _____ |
| sour | _____ |
| an additive | _____ |

## 7 DISCUSSION

Discuss the following questions in pairs or groups.

1 Which of the following describe you? Which do not describe you? "I like spicy food." "I have a sweet tooth." "I enjoy salty food." "I try not to eat food with MSG." Explain.

2 In your family, who is the best cook? Why is his or her cooking so good?

3 What foods do you think people will be eating a hundred years from now?

# CHAPTER
# 9
# Eat Less, Live Longer?

## 1 TOPIC PREVIEW

**A** Which of these food groups should you eat the most of? Which should you eat the least of? Number the food groups from 1 (the most) to 6 (the least). Share your answers with your classmates.

_____ whole grains

_____ meat, fish, and poultry

_____ fruit

_____ dairy products, such as milk and yogurt

_____ sweets, such as cake and cookies

_____ vegetables

**B** Read the title of this chapter, look at the picture, and discuss the following questions.

**1** Do you think there is a relationship between the foods you eat and your health?

**2** Do you usually read food labels? Why or why not?

**3** What do you think the reading is going to be about?

## 2 VOCABULARY PREVIEW

**A** Read the word lists. Put a check (✓) next to the words that you know and can use in a sentence. Compare your answers with a partner. Then look up any unfamiliar words in a dictionary.

| Food and Nutrition | Academic Word List | Biology |
| --- | --- | --- |
| calorie<br>diet (*n.*)<br>fast (*v.*) | benefit (*n.*)<br>consume<br>data<br>process (*n.*)<br>restrict<br>significantly | gene<br>lab animal<br>life expectancy |

The chart shows selected words from the reading related to food and nutrition, biology, and the Academic Word List (AWL). For more information about the AWL, see page 121.

**B** Fill in the blanks with words from Part A.

1 The _____ of humans has increased because of modern medicine.

2 The mouse is the most common _____ .

3 He is trying to lose weight, so he is counting every _____ .

4 A healthy _____ includes a lot of fruit and vegetables.

5 Losing weight takes a long time. It is a slow _____ .

6 Scientists analyze the _____ from their experiments.

7 People with red hair have a _____ that makes their hair red.

8 Young people usually _____ more candy than older people.

9 In some religions, people do not eat anything on certain days. They _____ .

10 They did a lot of exercise and ate less. Their health improved a lot. It improved _____ .

11 There is a health _____ to eating lots of fruits and vegetables.

12 Many parents _____ the amount of sugar their children eat.

Preview the questions in Reading Check Part A on page 68. Then read the story.

# Eat Less, Live Longer?

1    Owen and Canto live near each other. They lead similar lives and are close in age, but they look very different. Canto is strong and healthy. Owen, on the other hand, is slow and heavy. He is losing his hair, and he moves like an old man.

2    The biggest difference between Owen and Canto, however, is their life expectancy. Scientists expect Canto to live 30 percent longer than Owen. Why? Every day for 17 years, Canto has eaten a diet with many fewer calories than Owen. Scientists think this is the reason Canto does not have heart disease or diabetes,[1] common health problems in old age. It seems that eating less has kept Canto's body younger.

3    Owen and Canto are not people – they are monkeys. They live in a scientific research laboratory at the University of Wisconsin in the United States. Scientists at the lab are studying the effects of low-calorie diets. Does eating a diet with many fewer calories in it have health benefits? Does eating less also increase life expectancy?

4    Scientists in other laboratories around the world are doing similar research. So far, the results suggest the same thing. If you restrict the number of calories that an animal eats, it will live longer than an animal that eats a lot. In one study, mice ate 30 percent fewer calories than normal. These mice lived 40 percent longer than the mice that had a normal diet. They also had fewer age-related problems and diseases.

---

[1] *diabetes:* a disease in which the body cannot control the level of sugar in the blood

Scientists are beginning to understand the reason for the benefits    5
of eating less. When the body gets less food, the body produces a
substance called *sirtuin*. This substance acts on the genes in the body
that control aging. Sirtuin seems to slow down the aging process.

Humans, of course, are not lab animals. Will a very low-calorie    6
diet give humans the same health benefits as lab animals? Scientists
are beginning to study the effects of calorie restriction on humans,
too. In one study, scientists studied two groups of people for three
years. In the first group, people ate a normal diet. They consumed
between 2,000 and 3,500 calories a day. In the second group, people
ate a healthy, low-calorie diet. They consumed only 1,000 to 2,000
calories a day. After three years, the people in the second group were
significantly healthier. They had lowered their risk of diabetes and
heart disease.

Will eating fewer calories lead to a greater life expectancy for    7
humans? It will take scientists much longer to find this out. Humans
live much longer than laboratory animals, such as mice and monkeys.

There is a group of people, however, who already believe they will    8
live longer by eating less. They are members of the Calorie Restriction
Society. They have studied the data about
animals. They believe that restricting their
calories will increase their life expectancy
and help them live healthier lives. On some
days, they fast, and they rarely eat more than
2,000 calories a day.

*Dean Pomerleau, member of
the Calorie Restriction Society*

Scientists don't expect many people to    9
follow such an extreme diet. They also
don't expect a huge increase in human
life expectancy. Many scientists expect an
increase of about 9 percent, but others expect
only 2 percent. They believe the major benefit
of a low-calorie diet is a healthier, more active
life, as Canto the monkey has. A 90-year-old
may feel like a 65-year-old.

We are still waiting for scientists to tell us    10
if calorie restriction really works. So, the best
advice is to eat well. Just don't eat too much!

# 4 READING CHECK

**A** Are these statements true or false? Write *T* (true) or *F* (false).

1 _____ Canto and Owen both eat what they want.

2 _____ A low-calorie diet causes age-related diseases.

3 _____ People who eat less may have longer lives.

**B** Circle the letter of the best answer.

1 Owen and Canto _____ the same age.
   **a** are    **b** look    **c** are almost

2 Canto _____ common health problems of old age.
   **a** has many    **b** has some    **c** does not have

3 Researchers think _____ will live 30 percent longer on the low-calorie diet.
   **a** Owen    **b** Canto    **c** people

4 In a research study, mice on a restricted diet lived _____ longer than normal mice.
   **a** 20 percent    **b** 30 percent    **c** 40 percent

5 When does the body produce sirtuin?
   **a** all the time
   **b** when genes slow the body down
   **c** when the body does not have a lot of food

6 What was the difference between the two groups of people in the research study?
   **a** One group consumed only 500 calories per day.
   **b** One group was healthier at the end of the study.
   **c** One group was three years older.

7 Members of the Calorie Restriction Society _____ .
   **a** fast on some days
   **b** believe they will live 200 years
   **c** eat more than 2,000 calories per day

8 Scientists expect _____ if they consume fewer calories.
   **a** people will live 30 percent longer
   **b** people will live healthier lives
   **c** people will feel 60 years younger

## 5 VOCABULARY CHECK

**A** Retell the story. Fill in the blanks with the correct words from the box.

| | | | | |
|---|---|---|---|---|
| calories | consumed | data | diet | fast |
| lab animals | life expectancy | process | restriction | significantly |

Will you live longer if you eat less? Scientists are studying the relationship between a low-calorie _____ and _____ 
in animals. In one experiment, one group of mice _____ 
fewer _____ than a second group. The first group lived _____ longer than the second and appeared much healthier.

Scientists now want to know if there are benefits to people as well as to _____ . They are looking at the _____ 
from a research study involving humans. Members of the Calorie _____ Society eat a limited amount of very nutritious food. Some days they _____ instead of eating. Scientists think that a substance called *sirtuin* is more active when the body gets less food. Sirtuin may slow down the aging _____ . So does eating less help people live longer? Possibly. However, we still need to wait for scientists to do more research.

**B** Fill in the blanks with the correct form of the word.

| Verb | Noun | Adjective |
|---|---|---|
| benefit | benefit | beneficial |
| restrict | restriction | restricted |
| – | gene | genetic |

1 The color of your eyes is _____ .

2 A low-calorie diet may be _____ to people.

3 It is difficult to follow a _____ diet.

4 How does calorie restriction _____ people?

5 The doctor told the patient to _____ the amount of sugar he eats.

## 6 APPLYING READING SKILLS

> *Some readings contain mathematical information, especially percentages.*
> ***Understanding mathematical information*** *can lead to a deeper understanding*
> *of a reading.*

**A** Work with a partner. Read the questions below. Then go back to the text to find the information that you will need to answer the questions. The information in the box below the questions will help you calculate percentage increase or decrease.

**1** Monkeys usually live 27 years. To what age do scientists expect Canto to live?

**2** Mice usually live for 12 months. How many months do scientists expect the mice that ate fewer calories to live?

> **Working with percentages**
>
> 10% = .10     10% of 30 = (.10 x 30) = 3
>                   A 10% increase of 30 = 30 + (.10 x 30) = 33
>                   A 10% decrease of 30 = 30 − (.10 x 30) = 27

**B** Show your understanding of percentage data. Answer the questions below.

**1** Average life expectancy in the United States is 77 years. How long do scientists expect average Americans on low-calorie diets to live if they expect them to increase their life expectancy by 2 percent?

**2** How long do scientists expect average Americans on low-calorie diets to live if they expect them to increase their life expectancy by 9 percent?

**3** If a woman who normally eats 2,000 calories a day restricts her calories a day by 35 percent, how many calories a day will she eat?

## 7 DISCUSSION

Discuss the following questions in pairs or groups.

**1** Do you think scientists should use monkeys to do scientific experiments? Explain.

**2** Does the research make you want to restrict the number of calories you eat? Why or why not?

**3** In addition to having a healthy diet, what else can you do to increase your life expectancy?

## VOCABULARY REVIEW

| Chapter **7** | Chapter **8** | Chapter **9** |
|---|---|---|
| **Food and Nutrition** | **Food and Nutrition** | **Food and Nutrition** |
| mineral · nutritious · vitamin | additive · food chemist · seaweed | calorie · diet (*n.*) · fast (*v.*) |
| **Academic Word List** | **Academic Word List** | **Academic Word List** |
| expand · source · symbol | isolate · occur · physical · respond (to) | benefit (*n.*) · consume · data · process (*n.*) · restrict · significantly |
| **Agriculture** | **Culinary Arts** | **Biology** |
| crop · grow · harvest (*v.*) · import tax · plant (*v.*) · seed | chef · flavor (*v.*) · fry · ingredient · sauce | gene · lab animal · life expectancy |

Find words in the chart that match the definitions. Answers to 1–4 are from Chapter 7. Answers to 5–8 are from Chapter 8. Answers to 9–12 are from Chapter 9.

**1** To gather fruits or vegetables: _____

**2** Something used to represent something else: _____

**3** Describing food that makes your body healthy: _____

**4** Where something comes from: _____

**5** To cook food at a very high heat, usually in oil: _____

**6** A plant that comes from the sea: _____

**7** To separate something from other things: _____

**8** To add spices or other taste to food: _____

**9** A unit of energy in food: _____

**10** The average time that a group of people or animals will live:

_____

**11** To use something, for example, fuel, energy, or time: _____

**12** By a large amount: _____

## VOCABULARY IN USE

Work with a partner or small group, and discuss the questions below.

1 Do you have a good daily **diet**? Which nutritious foods do you eat frequently?

2 When you cook, what do you usually **flavor** your food with?

3 Do you think it is a good idea to take **vitamins**? Why or why not?

4 How much water do you usually **consume** in a day? Do you think it is a good idea to drink a lot of water? Why or why not?

5 Do you or people you know ever **fast**? For what reasons?

6 Which **physical** activities do you do regularly?

7 Did your parents **restrict** any of your activities when you were a child? Explain.

8 Have you ever **planted** a **seed**? Describe the **process**.

## ROLE PLAY

Work with a partner. Student A is a nutritionist, an expert in nutrition. Student B does not feel healthy and wants advice about how to feel better. Student A asks Student B questions and then gives suggestions. When you finish, change roles.

## WRITING

Write a persuasive paragraph in which you give suggestions for improving the typical diet where you live. Consider the following questions.

- Why is it important for people to change the way they eat?
- What changes can people make to have healthier eating habits?
- What foods can people eat to be healthier?
- What are some ways to make healthy food delicious so that people want to eat it?

## WEBQUEST

Find more information about the topics in this unit by going on the Internet. Go to www.cambridge.org/readthis and follow the instructions for doing a WebQuest. Search for facts. Have fun. Good luck!

# Criminal Justice

## Chapter 10

### Teenage Con Man

Frank Abagnale was no ordinary teenager. He tricked people in 26 countries.

**Content areas:**
- Criminal Justice
- Banking

## Chapter 11

### Fingerprints Don't Lie – Or Do They?

Henry Faulds was a doctor, not a police officer, but his work helped police all over the world.

**Content areas:**
- Criminal Justice
- Information Systems

## Chapter 12

### "I Then . . ."

It took 45 years and computer technology to help Derek Bentley's family prove his innocence.

**Content areas:**
- Criminal Justice
- Language Studies

# 10
# Teenage Con Man

## 1 TOPIC PREVIEW

**A** People do not write checks as much now as they used to. Put a check (✓) next to the ways people usually use checks today. Share your answers with your classmates.

**1** _____ to pay people who work for you

**2** _____ to pay your telephone bill

**3** _____ to buy things in stores

**4** _____ to get money from the bank

**5** _____ _____ (your idea)

**B** Read the title of this chapter, look at the picture, and discuss the following questions.

**1** A *con man* is someone who tricks people and steals their money. How can someone do that?

**2** How do people who work in banks know that a check is real? How can people who work in stores or hotels be sure that a check is good?

**3** What do you think the reading is going to be about?

# 2 VOCABULARY PREVIEW

**A** Read the word lists. Put a check (✓) next to the words that you know and can use in a sentence. Compare your answers with a partner. Then look up any unfamiliar words in a dictionary.

| Criminal Justice | Academic Word List | Banking |
|---|---|---|
| **criminal** (*n.*)<br>**forge**<br>**fraud**<br>**prison**<br>(go on) **trial** | **expert**<br>**identity**<br>**obviously** | (bank) **account**<br>**cash** (a check) (*v.*)<br>**charge** (*v.*)<br>**deposit** (a check) (*v.*) |

The chart shows selected words from the reading related to criminal justice, banking, and the Academic Word List (AWL). For more information about the AWL, see page 121.

**B** Fill in the blanks with words from Part A.

**1** She knows more than anyone else. She is a/an _____ .

**2** They _____ ten dollars a day for parking.

**3** He is always doing crazy things, but he always obeys the laws. He isn't a/an _____ .

**4** When I get paid, I put the money in my bank _____ .

**5** Who is he? I don't know his _____ .

**6** I _____ money in the bank once a month.

**7** He used a special printer to _____ dollar bills.

**8** When people need money, they can go to the bank to _____ a check.

**9** The police arrested him. Three months later, he went on _____ for the crime.

**10** This is _____ not my handwriting. I don't know who wrote this.

**11** He stole money, so he went to _____ for five years.

**12** She used a trick to get money from people. This is _____ .

Preview the questions in Reading Check Part A on page 78. Then read the story.

# Teenage Con Man

*Leonardo DiCaprio (left) and Frank Abagnale[1]*

1    Frank Abagnale was leaving his hotel. He wore the uniform of an airline pilot. He didn't have to pay for his room or his meals because the hotel charged them all to the airline. At the front desk, he asked the manager to cash a paycheck[2] for him. "Of course, sir!" The hotel manager was happy to cash the airline's check.

2    A few weeks later, however, the hotel manager was not so happy. Abagnale was not a pilot. He did not work for the airline. The paycheck was not real. Frank Abagnale was a con man.

3    Abagnale started his career as a criminal in New York in the 1960s. He was just a teenager, but he looked much older. He opened accounts at different banks. Then he bought things in stores and paid for them with checks from these accounts. The accounts didn't have enough money in them to cover the checks, but the stores didn't know this. By the time they realized it, Abagnale was using a different bank.

4    Abagnale was very smart. After a while, he taught himself to forge checks. Then he deposited these fake checks. One day, he was filling

---

[1] Leonardo DiCaprio played Frank Abagnale in the movie *Catch Me if You Can.*
[2] *paycheck:* a check that a company gives to pay employees for their work

out a deposit slip[3] at a bank and he got a new idea. He took a few of the deposit slips home. He typed his own account number on the forms. Then he took them back to the bank, and he put them with the other deposit slips for customers to use. When customers used the deposit slips, their money went into Abagnale's account.

Obviously, Abagnale had to move from city to city as banks discovered his tricks. When he was just 16, he created his identity as an airline pilot. As a pilot, he didn't have to pay for air travel. He could also stay at hotels where other pilots stayed without paying. He never actually flew a plane, but he got on over 250 flights and stayed at hotels all over the world at the airline's expense. He created false paychecks and cashed them.

Sometimes Abagnale had to change identities so that the police would not catch him. Once he pretended to be a doctor. He even worked in a hospital in Atlanta. Another time, he pretended to have a law degree from Harvard University. He got a job in a law office in New Orleans, but one of the lawyers there – a real Harvard graduate – started asking Abagnale a lot of questions. It was time to be a pilot again!

By the time he was 21, Abagnale's face was on "Most Wanted" posters[4] in 26 different countries. Someone recognized him in France and called the police. Abagnale spent six months in a French prison. Then he went on trial in Sweden, where he spent another six months in prison. At his trial in the United States, he got 12 years in prison. However, Abagnale was a prisoner in the United States for only five years. He got out of prison for good behavior, but he had trouble finding a good job because of his criminal past. He finally went to a bank and offered to teach the bank workers about different kinds of fraud. He told them, "If you don't learn from me, you don't have to pay me." Of course, they learned a lot from him, and Abagnale started his new career as a fraud expert. After all, he knows both sides of the business.

[3] *deposit slip:* a small form you fill out when you put money in a bank
[4] *"Most Wanted" poster:* a poster with pictures of important criminals. The poster is put in public places, such as post offices.

# 4 READING CHECK

**A** Are these statements true or false? Write *T* (true) or *F* (false).

1 _____ Frank Abagnale was an airline pilot.

2 _____ Frank Abagnale was very smart but not honest.

3 _____ Frank Abagnale never went to prison in the United States.

**B** Circle the letter of the best answer.

1 What was Abagnale's earliest crime?
   **a** writing bad checks
   **b** leaving a hotel without paying
   **c** pretending to be an airline pilot

2 Abagnale stole money from other people when he _____ .
   **a** took their paychecks
   **b** took money out of their bank accounts
   **c** put his account number on deposit slips at the bank

3 When Abagnale pretended to be a pilot, he _____ .
   **a** flew planes 250 different times
   **b** paid his hotel bills with fake money
   **c** forged and cashed airline paychecks

4 Which of these statements is *not* true?
   **a** The airline paid for Abagnale's hotels.
   **b** Pilots didn't have to pay for their tickets.
   **c** The airline paid Abagnale a lot of money.

5 What was a big advantage for Abagnale?
   **a** He knew how to fly.
   **b** His father was a banker.
   **c** He looked older than his age.

6 Where did Abagnale pretend to be a doctor?
   **a** New York     **b** Atlanta     **c** New Orleans

7 How much time did Abagnale actually spend in prison?
   **a** 6 years     **b** 12 years     **c** 13 years

8 Bank managers now think of Abagnale as a _____ .
   **a** fraud expert     **b** con man     **c** prisoner

## 5 VOCABULARY CHECK

**A** Retell the story. Fill in the blanks with the correct words from the box.

| accounts | cashed | charged | criminal |
|----------|--------|---------|----------|
| deposit | expert | forge | fraud |
| identity | obviously | prison | trial |

Frank Abagnale became a/an _____ when he was just
                                          1
a teenager. He opened _____ at different banks. He wrote
                               2
checks even though he did not have money in those banks. He even put his

account number on the banks' _____ slips. When bank
                                          3
customers used the slips, their money went into Abagnale's accounts. He

also taught himself how to _____ checks. Soon the police
                                   4
were looking for Abagnale, so he took on a new _____ as
                                                         5
an airline pilot. As a pilot, Abagnale _____ his hotel and
                                               6
meal bills to the airline. He also created and _____ false
                                                        7
paychecks from the airline.

Finally, the police caught Abagnale. He spent time in

_____ in both Sweden and France. Then he went on
        8
_____ in the United States. After five years in a U.S.
        9
prison, Abagnale established a new and very successful career teaching

banks how to identify _____ . _____ ,
                              10                    11
he knows a lot about it. This con man was a real _____ !
                                                         12

**B** Some words often appear together. Circle the words that often appear with the
words in bold.

| | | | | |
|---|---|---|---|---|
| 1 | **to forge** | a bank | a check | a job |
| 2 | **a bank** | account | identity | bill |
| 3 | **to cash** | money | a check | a charge |
| 4 | **to charge** | my hotel room | cash | a check |
| 5 | **an expert** | business | meal | opinion |

## 6 APPLYING READING SKILLS

> ***Finding the main ideas and supporting details*** *in a reading is an important skill. Supporting details explain the main ideas more fully and will help you have a better understanding of a reading.*

**A** Write *M* next to the two sentences that are main ideas. Write *S* next to the sentences that give supporting details. Match the *S* sentences to the *M* sentences they support. All of the sentences are about Frank Abagnale.

**1** _____ He forged checks.

**2** _____ He used different identities.

**3** _____ He left deposit slips in the bank with his account number filled in.

**4** _____ He worked in a hospital.

**5** _____ He thought of different ways to make money illegally.

**6** _____ He pretended to be a pilot.

**B** Find two details from the text that support each main idea.

| MAIN IDEA | SUPPORTING DETAILS |
|---|---|
| **1** Frank Abagnale spent many years paying for his life of crime. | ▪ <br> ▪ |
| **2** Frank Abagnale's last job was the perfect job for him! | ▪ <br> ▪ |

## 7 DISCUSSION

Discuss the following questions in pairs or groups.

**1** Abagnale wrote bad checks, put his account number on deposit slips in banks, and created fake paychecks in the 1960s. Would it be possible to do this now? Why or why not?

**2** Imagine you are a bank manager. Would you ask Abagnale to train your workers to find fraud? Why or why not?

**3** Do you know of any other famous examples of fraud? Explain.

CHAPTER

# 11

---

# Fingerprints Don't Lie – Or Do They?

## 1 TOPIC PREVIEW

**A** How do the police use the following to help them solve crimes? Share your ideas with your classmates.

1 handwriting

2 teeth

3 fingerprints

4 blood

5 (your idea)

**B** Read the title of this chapter, look at the picture, and discuss the following questions.

1 Are fingerprints a good way to identify criminals? Why or why not?
2 What other ways can you think of for people to use fingerprints?
3 What do you think the reading is going to be about?

## 2 VOCABULARY PREVIEW

**A** Read the word lists. Put a check (✓) next to the words that you know and can use in a sentence. Compare your answers with a partner. Then look up any unfamiliar words in a dictionary.

| Criminal Justice | Academic Word List | Information Systems |
|---|---|---|
| arrest (*v.*)<br>guilty<br>innocent<br>suspect (*n.*)<br>theft | identical<br>investigate<br>unique | classify<br>(search a) database<br>match (*v.*)<br>record (*n.*) |

The chart shows selected words from the reading related to criminal justice, information systems, and the Academic Word List (AWL). For more information about the AWL, see page 121.

**B** Fill in the blanks with words from Part A.

**1** The signatures on the two checks looked exactly the same. They were _____ .

**2** The two sets of fingerprints were different. They did not _____ .

**3** When police find a criminal, they _____ him or her.

**4** There was a/an _____ from her car. Someone stole her camera.

**5** Police believe my neighbor robbed a bank. He is a/an _____ .

**6** We keep the information on the computer, and it is easy to search because it is in a/an _____ .

**7** Police officers began to _____ the murder.

**8** She stole the money. She was _____ of the crime.

**9** There is no one like you. You are _____ .

**10** Police _____ crimes into different types. They keep files for each type.

**11** The man did not commit the crime. He is _____ .

**12** There is no information in our files about that. There is no _____ .

Preview the questions in Reading Check Part A on page 85. Then read the story.

# Fingerprints Don't Lie – Or Do They?

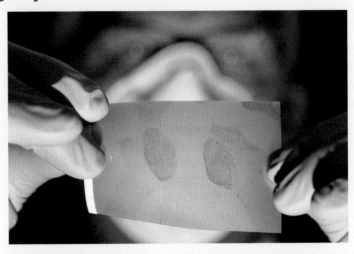

In 1892 in Argentina, a police officer named Juan Vucetich was 1
investigating the murder of two people. At the scene of the crime,[1] he
saw a mark on a door. It was a fingerprint! He compared this to the
prints of two suspects in the murder. One of the fingerprints matched,
and Vucetich solved the crime. What was so unusual about this? It was
the first time a fingerprint was used to solve a murder.

In ancient times, people used fingerprints to identify people. They 2
also used them as signatures in business. However, no one used
fingerprints in crime work until the late 1880s. Three men, working
in three different areas of the world, made this possible.

The first man who collected a large number of fingerprints was 3
William Herschel. He worked for the British government in India. He
took fingerprints when people signed official papers. For many years,
he collected the same people's fingerprints several times. He made an
important discovery. Fingerprints do not change over time.

At about the same time, a Scottish doctor in Japan began to study 4
fingerprints. Henry Faulds was looking at ancient Japanese pottery[2]
one day when he noticed small lines on the pots. It occurred to him
that the lines were 2,000-year-old fingerprints. Faulds wondered, "Are
fingerprints unique to each person?" He began to take fingerprints

---

[1] *scene of the crime:* place where the crime happened
[2] *pottery:* objects, such as bowls, made of baked clay

of all his friends, co-workers, and students at his medical school. Each print was unique. He also wondered, "Can you change your fingerprints?" He shaved the fingerprints off his fingers with a razor to find out. Would they grow back the same? They did.

5　　One day, there was a theft in Faulds's medical school. Some alcohol was missing. Faulds found fingerprints on the bottle. He compared the fingerprints to the ones in his records, and he found a match. The thief was one of his medical students. By examining fingerprints, Faulds solved the crime.

6　　Both Herschel and Faulds collected fingerprints, but there was a problem. It was very difficult to use their collections to identify a specific fingerprint. Francis Galton in England made it easier. He noticed common patterns[3] in fingerprints. He used these to help classify fingerprints. These features, called "Galton details," made it easier for police to search through fingerprint records. The system is still in use today. When police find a fingerprint, they look at the Galton details. Then they search for other fingerprints with similar features.

7　　Like Faulds, Galton believed that each person had a unique fingerprint. According to Galton, the chance of two people with the same fingerprint was 1 in 64 billion. Even the fingerprints of identical twins are different. Fingerprints were the perfect tool to identify criminals.

8　　For more than 100 years, no one found two people with the same prints. Then, in 2004, terrorists committed[4] a crime in Madrid, Spain. Police in Madrid found a fingerprint. They used computers to search databases of fingerprint records all over the world. Three fingerprint experts agreed that a man on the West Coast of the United States was one of the criminals. Police arrested him, but the experts were wrong. The man was innocent. Another man was guilty. Amazingly, the two men who were 6,000 miles away from each other had fingerprints that were almost exactly identical.

*A scientist examines a fingerprint database.*

9　　After the mistake made by the experts in the Madrid case, the police have to be very careful. Today, millions and millions of fingerprints are in databases. Many of them are almost identical. However, unless they are exactly identical, each one is still unique!

---

[3] *pattern:* a regular series of shapes
[4] *commit:* to do something wrong or illegal

# 4 READING CHECK

**A** Match the event to the name of the country.

1 The first murder case was solved using fingerprinting.
   **a** Argentina    **b** Japan    **c** India

2 William Herschel collected fingerprints while working for the British government.
   **a** Japan    **b** India    **c** England

3 Francis Galton developed the first system for classifying fingerprints.
   **a** India    **b** England    **c** Argentina

**B** Circle the letter of the best answer.

1 Who solved the first murder using fingerprinting?
   **a** Juan Vucetich    **b** William Herschel    **c** Henry Faulds

2 How long have fingerprints been used as a way to identify people?
   **a** since ancient times    **b** since the 1880s    **c** since 2004

3 Where did Dr. Faulds find 2,000-year-old fingerprints?
   **a** on ancient pottery    **b** on a bottle of alcohol    **c** on a doorway

4 When Dr. Faulds shaved off his fingerprints, they _____ .
   **a** changed    **b** disappeared    **c** grew back the same

5 How did Dr. Faulds solve a crime at his medical school?
   **a** He matched fingerprints.
   **b** He asked students.
   **c** He looked for the alcohol.

6 In what way did Francis Galton change the field of fingerprinting?
   **a** He identified a criminal from a fingerprint.
   **b** He classified fingerprints.
   **c** He collected a lot of fingerprints.

7 Who had almost identical fingerprints?
   **a** Dr. Faulds and Galton
   **b** two criminals
   **c** a criminal and an innocent man

8 Who was one of the criminals in the Madrid crime?
   **a** a person from Madrid
   **b** a person from the United States
   **c** The story does not say.

# 5 VOCABULARY CHECK

**A** Retell the story. Fill in the blanks with the correct words from the box.

| classify | databases | guilty | identical | innocent |
| investigate | matches | suspect | theft | unique |

Today, there are many computer _____ full of
fingerprints. When the police _____ a crime scene, they
_____ 2
collect fingerprints. Then they try to find out if one of the fingerprints
_____ the fingerprints of a/an _____ .
_____3                                              _____4
If the police don't find a person's fingerprints at a crime scene, the person
is probably _____ .
_____5

Three men were helpful in the development of using fingerprints for
police work. In India, William Herschel found that fingerprints never change
over time. In Japan, Dr. Henry Faulds also studied fingerprints. There was
a/an _____ in Dr. Faulds's medical school, and Faulds
_____6
used a fingerprint to find the _____ person. In England, a
_____7
third man, named Francis Galton, created a way to _____
_____8
fingerprints into types. Galton believed that each person's fingerprints were
_____ . However, now we know that it is possible for two
_____9
people to have fingerprints that are almost _____ .
_____10

**B** Some words have the same form for the noun and the verb. How are the
underlined words used in these sentences? Circle *noun* or *verb*.

1 Why did they <u>arrest</u> him?                    noun    verb

2 The police decided to <u>record</u> her answer.    noun    verb

3 No one knew about his <u>arrest</u>.               noun    verb

4 He was the only <u>suspect</u> at first.           noun    verb

5 The fingerprints did not <u>match</u>.             noun    verb

6 Do the police <u>suspect</u> her?                  noun    verb

7 We have no <u>record</u> of her birth.             noun    verb

## 6 APPLYING READING SKILLS

> *Organizing information into a chart* can help you see the information in a reading in a new way. This can give you a deeper understanding of the reading. It can also help you remember the details of a reading when you have to prepare for a test.

**A** Complete the chart. Write the information below in the correct columns.

- 1892
- Compared fingerprint with prints of two suspects
- Dr. Henry Faulds
- Japan
- Matched fingerprints with records
- Argentina
- 1880s
- Juan Vucetich

|  | MURDER OF TWO PEOPLE | ALCOHOL STOLEN FROM LAB |
|---|---|---|
| *Where?* |  |  |
| *When?* |  |  |
| *Who?* |  |  |
| *How?* |  |  |

**B** Practice taking notes in the chart below. Use information from the reading.

|  | TERRORIST CASE |
|---|---|
| *Where?* |  |
| *When?* |  |
| *Who?* |  |
| *How?* |  |

## 7 DISCUSSION

Discuss the following questions in pairs or groups.

1 After the Madrid case, do you believe that police should use fingerprints as evidence? Why or why not?

2 Today, what do criminals do so that they don't leave fingerprints at crime scenes?

3 What can police do now to catch criminals that they couldn't do 50 years ago?

## 1  TOPIC PREVIEW

**A**  Imagine this crime. A 16-year-old boy goes with a 19-year-old boy to rob a store. The 16-year-old boy kills a policeman during the crime. What should happen to each boy? Check (✓) your answers below. Share your answers with your classmates.

Age:  Age:
16    19

**1** _____ _____ one year in prison

**2** _____ _____ ten years in prison

**3** _____ _____ life in prison

**4** _____ _____ the death penalty (the government kills him)

**5** _____ _____ _____ _____ (your idea)

**B**  Read the title of this chapter, look at the picture, and discuss the following questions.

**1** Describe the picture. What is happening? What are the people wearing?

**2** What country do you think this is in? What makes you think that?

**3** What do you think the reading is going to be about?

## 2 VOCABULARY PREVIEW

**A** Read the word lists. Put a check (✓) next to the words that you know and can use in a sentence. Compare your answers with a partner. Then look up any unfamiliar words in a dictionary.

| Criminal Justice | Academic Word List | Language Studies |
|---|---|---|
| accuse<br>court<br>judge (*n.*)<br>jury<br>verdict | adult<br>analysis<br>evidence | linguist<br>statement<br>subject (of a sentence)<br>usage |

The chart shows selected words from the reading related to criminal justice, language studies, and the Academic Word List (AWL). For more information about the AWL, see page 121.

**B** Write the word from Part A next to its definition.

1 The place where trials happen: _____

2 To say that someone is responsible for a crime or has done something wrong: _____

3 The way people actually speak and write a language: _____

4 Someone who is over 18 years old: _____

5 The person or thing that performs the action of a verb:

_____

6 A decision in a trial about whether someone is guilty: _____

7 The study of something in an organized way: _____

8 Anything that helps to prove that something is or is not true:

_____

9 Something that is said or written officially as a record:

_____

10 A group of people who listen to the facts of a trial and decide whether a person is guilty or not guilty: _____

11 Someone who studies the structure of language: _____

12 A person who is in charge of a trial: _____

Preview the questions in Reading Check Part A on page 92. Then read the story.

# "I Then..."

Bentley's niece at his grave (left); Bentley, age 19 (right)

1    In 1952, a British court found Derek Bentley guilty in the murder of a police officer. Was he really guilty? His family didn't think so. For many years, they tried to clear his name! Finally, a linguist and a computer helped them do that.

2    Bentley was a slow learner. He couldn't even write his name. On the night of the murder, Bentley was 19. He was with his 16-year-old friend, Christopher Craig. Craig wanted Bentley to help him rob a warehouse? Someone saw them and called the police. Craig had a gun. When the policemen arrived, Craig shot and killed one of them.

3    Craig was accused of murder. Bentley was also accused of murder because he was with Craig. In the trial, the police presented a statement by Derek Bentley as evidence. The police said in court that the statement contained Bentley's exact words. This police evidence helped the jury find Bentley guilty. Bentley and Craig both said the police were lying. Almost 50 years later, a professor of linguistics named Malcolm Coulthard was able to show that Bentley and Craig were probably right.

4    Coulthard uses his knowledge of language to help solve crimes. Coulthard studied the statement. He noticed something interesting

---

¹ *clear someone's name:* to prove that someone is not guilty of something that he or she was accused of

² *warehouse:* a building to store things before they are used or sold

about the use of the word *then*. He did research with the help of a computer. This is what he found:

| Use of *then* . . . | Rate of use . . . |
|---|---|
| In normal conversation | Once in every 500 words |
| By police officers | Once in every 78 words |
| In Bentley's statement | Once in every 58 words |

Coulthard also noticed something else. Most people use *then* before the subject of the sentence. They say "Then I . . ." In Bentley's statement, however, *then* usually followed the subject.

| Word order in Bentley's statement | Normal word order |
|---|---|
| *I then* ran after them . . . | *Then I* ran after them . . . |
| *Chris then* jumped over and . . . | *Then Chris* jumped over and . . . |
| *Chris then* climbed up . . . | *Then Chris* climbed up . . . |

Coulthard did more research on his computer. He looked at the way people use "I then." Here are the results of his research: Police officers use the word order "I then" very often. They use it once in every 119 words. Other people use "I then" only once in every 165,000 words. **5**

All of Coulthard's research showed that the speech pattern in Bentley's statement was similar to police usage of the word *then*. This evidence suggested that the words in the statement were not Bentley's words. Police officers wrote the statement. **6**

Malcolm Coulthard

In 1998, a British judge changed the verdict. One piece of evidence was Coulthard's linguistic analysis of Bentley's statement. Linguistics helped Bentley's family get justice. Unfortunately, it was 45 years too late for Bentley. Christopher Craig, at 16, was a juvenile.[3] He went to prison for 10 years. Bentley, at 19, was an adult. He was hanged[4] in 1953. **7**

---

[3] *juvenile:* a young person; not an adult for legal purposes
[4] *hanged:* put to death using a rope around the neck

## 4 READING CHECK

**A** Match the name of the person to the description.

1 _____ Derek Bentley    **a** a young man who shot a policeman

2 _____ Christopher Craig    **b** a linguist who analyzes language to solve crimes

3 _____ Malcolm Coulthard    **c** a slow learner who was hanged for murder

**B** Circle the letter of the best answer.

1 What problem did Derek Bentley have?
   **a** He was 16.    **b** He had difficulty learning.    **c** He did not have friends.

2 What happened in 1952?
   **a** A linguistics professor proved that Bentley was innocent of murder.
   **b** A court decided that Bentley was guilty of murder.
   **c** Bentley's family cleared his name.

3 Which of these statements is *not* true?
   **a** Bentley shot the police officer.
   **b** The police said Craig murdered a police officer.
   **c** The police used a statement as evidence.

4 Why was Bentley with Craig on the night of the murder?
   **a** They were looking for a house to rob.
   **b** Craig asked Bentley to help him rob a warehouse.
   **c** Bentley wanted Craig to help him rob a warehouse.

5 Why did almost 50 years pass before Coulthard could produce linguistic evidence?
   **a** The police lost Bentley's original statement.
   **b** Bentley asked for help getting out of jail.
   **c** Coulthard needed modern computer technology to analyze language.

6 What was unusual about Bentley's official statement?
   **a** It used the word *then* less often than normal.
   **b** It used the word *then* only at the beginning of sentences.
   **c** It used the word *then* in the same way as police officers do.

7 What happened in 1998?
   **a** Bentley got out of jail.
   **b** A judge changed Bentley's guilty verdict.
   **c** Craig was sent to prison for the murder.

8 Which person was a juvenile?
   **a** Derek Bentley    **b** Christopher Craig    **c** Malcolm Coulthard

## 5 VOCABULARY CHECK

**A** Retell the story. Fill in the blanks with the correct words from the box.

| | | | |
|---|---|---|---|
| accused | adult | analysis | court |
| evidence | judge | jury | linguist |
| statement | subject | usage | verdict |

Derek Bentley was _____ of the murder of a
police officer. In _____ , police presented a/an
_____ from Bentley as _____ . The
_____ decided that Bentley was guilty of murder.
Bentley's family disagreed with the _____ and worked for
years to show he was innocent.

Finally, Malcolm Coulthard, a/an _____ , got involved
in the case, and he studied Bentley's language. Coulthard compared the
language _____ of police to the way other people used
language. Coulthard's _____ showed some interesting
facts. Police used *then* after the _____ of a sentence more
often than other people. In 1998, a British _____ decided
Bentley's trial was not fair. However, it was too late for Bentley. As a/an
_____ , he had received the hardest punishment 45 years
earlier: death by hanging.

**B** Circle *a* or *b* to show which word belongs in each group.

| 1 | jury | court | **a** linguist | **b** judge |
|---|---|---|---|---|
| 2 | subject | linguist | **a** adult | **b** usage |
| 3 | trial | evidence | **a** verdict | **b** subject |
| 4 | accuse | judge | **a** analysis | **b** evidence |
| 5 | statement | evidence | **a** court | **b** adult |

# 6 APPLYING READING SKILLS

*When you read, you often learn new information.* **Applying information from a reading** *to new situations shows that you really understand the information well.*

**A** Use information from the reading to answer the following questions.

1 How often do most people use *then* in conversation?

_____

2 What word order do police usually use – *then I* or *I then*?

_____

3 How often do most people use *I then*? _____

**B** Practice applying information from the reading. Use the information above to answer these questions: Which of the people below are probably police? Which are probably not police? Put a check (✓) in the box.

|  | POLICE | NOT POLICE |
|---|---|---|
| 1 This person used 10,000 words and used the word *then* 20 times. |  |  |
| 2 This person said, "She then went into the house and closed the door." |  |  |
| 3 This person used 2,000 words and used the phrase *I then* 21 times. |  |  |
| 4 This person said, "Then, about ten minutes later, Mr. and Mrs. Smith got into their car and drove away." |  |  |
| 5 This person used 60,000 words and used the word *then* 750 times. |  |  |

# 7 DISCUSSION

Discuss the following questions in pairs or groups.

1 Why do you think the police changed Bentley's statement?
2 Why do you think Bentley's family worked so hard to prove he didn't commit murder?
3 Do you think people are often wrongly found guilty of crimes? Why or why not?

## VOCABULARY REVIEW

| Chapter **10** | Chapter **11** | Chapter **12** |
|---|---|---|
| **Criminal Justice** | **Criminal Justice** | **Criminal Justice** |
| **criminal** (*n.*) · **forge** · **fraud** · **prison** · (go on) **trial** | **arrest** (*v.*) · **guilty** · **innocent** · **suspect** (*n.*) · **theft** | **accuse** · **court** · **judge** (*n.*) · **jury** · **verdict** |
| **Academic Word List** | **Academic Word List** | **Academic Word List** |
| **expert** · **identity** · **obviously** | **identical** · **investigate** · **unique** | **adult** · **analysis** · **evidence** |
| **Banking** | **Information Systems** | **Language Studies** |
| (bank) **account** · **cash** (a check) (*v.*) · **charge** (*v.*) · **deposit** (a check) (*v.*) | **classify** · (search a) **database** · **match** (*v.*) · **record** (*n.*) | **linguist** · **statement** · **subject** (of a sentence) · **usage** |

Find words in the chart that match the definitions. Answers to 1–4 are from Chapter 10. Answers to 5–8 are from Chapter 11. Answers to 9–12 are from Chapter 12.

1  To buy something and agree to pay for it later: _____

2  To put an amount of money into a bank: _____

3  A person who knows a lot about something: _____

4  To make an illegal copy in order to trick people: _____

5  Only one of its type; unusual: _____

6  Someone who might be responsible for a crime: _____

7  To divide things into groups according to type: _____

8  Exactly the same: _____

9  The study of something in an organized way: _____

10  To say that someone is responsible for a crime: _____

11  The way people actually speak and write a language: _____

12  Anything that helps to prove that something is or is not true:

_____

# VOCABULARY IN USE

Work with a partner or small group, and discuss the questions below.

1 Do you have a bank **account**? Do you have a credit card **account**? What do you use each one for?

2 Do you keep a careful **record** of the money you save and spend? Why or why not?

3 Did you or your family **investigate** prices and products the last time you bought an expensive item such as a computer or a refrigerator? Explain.

4 Have you ever been to an interesting **trial** or seen one on TV? What happened? Why was it interesting?

5 Would you like to be a **judge**? Why or why not?

6 Would you like to serve on a **jury**? Why or why not?

7 At what age do you think someone becomes an **adult**?

8 Do you think a person who is 16 years old should go to **prison** if he or she commits a crime?

# ROLE PLAY

Work with a partner. Student A is a witness to a crime. You saw a man rob a customer who was coming out of a bank. Think of details such as the time of day, the robber's appearance, and the sequence of events. Student B is a police investigator. The police investigator asks the witness questions. When you finish, change roles and create a new crime scene.

# WRITING

Imagine you are a crime scene investigator. Write a one- or two-paragraph report about a crime scene. Include the following information in your report.

- Describe the crime scene. (a hotel room? a car? a bank? other?)

- What evidence did the criminal leave behind? (papers? fingerprints? clothing? other?)

- What do you think happened?

- How can you use the evidence to find the criminal?

# WEBQUEST

Find more information about the topics in this unit by going on the Internet. Go to www.cambridge.org/readthis and follow the instructions for doing a WebQuest. Search for facts. Have fun. Good luck!

# Psychology

## Chapter 13

### Death by Internet

We don't usually think of the Internet as a danger, but perhaps we should.

**Content areas:**
- Psychology
- Technology

## Chapter 14

### The Power of the Mind

People can do amazing things when they put their minds to it.

**Content areas:**
- Psychology
- Sports and Fitness

## Chapter 15

### Miracle on the Hudson

An airplane pilot with just the right skills saved 155 lives.

**Content areas:**
- Psychology
- Aviation

# CHAPTER
## 13
# Death by Internet

## 1 TOPIC PREVIEW

**A** Which of these things do you spend the most time doing on the Internet? Number them from 1 (most often) to 5 (least often). Share your answers with your classmates.

_____ sending and receiving e-mail

_____ doing research

_____ shopping

_____ playing online games

_____ _____ (your idea)

**B** Read the title of this chapter, look at the picture, and discuss the following questions.

**1** Do you think people can have health problems because they spend a lot of time on the Internet? Why or why not?

**2** How much time do you spend on the Internet each week? Do you think this is too much, or is it all right? Explain.

**3** What do you think the reading is going to be about?

# 2 VOCABULARY PREVIEW

**A** Read the word lists. Put a check (✓) next to the words that you know and can use in a sentence. Compare your answers with a partner. Then look up any unfamiliar words in a dictionary.

| Psychology | Academic Word List | Technology |
|---|---|---|
| addicted (to)<br>counseling<br>disorder | (have) **access** (to)<br>authority<br>collapse (v.)<br>estimate (v.)<br>generation<br>role | cyber café<br>virtual reality<br>wired |

The chart shows selected words from the reading related to psychology, technology, and the Academic Word List (AWL). For more information about the AWL, see page 121.

**B** Fill in the blanks with words from Part A.

1 We don't know the exact number. We have to _____ .

2 Teachers play an important _____ in a young person's life.

3 High school students meet with an advisor for _____ about what colleges to apply to.

4 This type of small restaurant serves some food and drinks, but most people go there to use the computers. It is a/an _____ .

5 It looks real, but it is all on computer. It is _____ .

6 My friends and I are all about the same age. We are from the same _____ .

7 He sees the wrong letters when he reads. He has a reading _____ .

8 If it's very hot and you don't drink water, you might _____ .

9 I can't go online. I don't have _____ to the Internet right now.

10 Some people must have soda every day. They are _____ to it.

11 He is a/an _____ on the subject of computers.

12 You can get on the Internet in this school. The school is _____ .

## 3 READING

Preview the questions in Reading Check Part A on page 102. Then read the story.

# Death by Internet

Cyber café in Hong Kong

1　　After 86 hours of playing his favorite online game, Kim Kyung-jae, a 24-year-old South Korean, collapsed and died. Ten days later in Fengyuan, Taiwan, 28-year-old Lien Wen-cheng walked into a cyber café and began to play. Thirty-six hours later, he left on a stretcher.[1] When the ambulance arrived at the hospital, Lien Wen-cheng was dead. What was the cause of his death? Heart failure. This was the medical explanation. Some people have another way to describe it. They call it "death by Internet."

2　　These deaths made people pay attention. The young men played for hours and hours without a break. They could not stop playing. Were they addicted to the Internet?

3　　Some experts say that we are in the middle of a global experiment. We will not know all the effects of long periods of Internet use for many years. Psychologists say the hours of Internet use are not the only problem. They are also asking questions about the role of the

---

[1] *stretcher:* a type of bed that medics use to carry people in emergencies

Internet in young people's lives. How is their schoolwork? Do they have good grades? Are they still playing sports? Do they have friends? An even more important question is, Are they upset when they cannot go online?

Jin, a teenager, used to go online after school. He ate dinner with his family, did homework, and got a good night's sleep. One day he got involved in an online game. He didn't stop playing to have dinner. He didn't do his homework. His focus all night was only on the virtual reality in the game. The next day, in the real world, he did poorly on a test. His parents took away his computer for a week. Jin became very angry. He refused to leave his room, and he refused to attend school. Jin's once-normal Internet use was now an addiction. 4

Parents like Jin's know there is a problem, but governments are also getting involved. China may be the first country to recognize Internet Addiction Disorder (IAD). Recent reports suggest that 13.7 percent of young Internet users in China (about 10 million) might have this disorder. In South Korea, too, the government sees Internet addiction as one of its most serious public health issues. South Korea is one of the most wired countries in the world. Ninety percent of the population has high-speed Internet access at home, and there are thousands of cyber cafés open 24 hours a day. Authorities in South Korea estimate that the average high school student spends as many as 23 hours per week playing online games. They also estimate that there are hundreds of thousands of children who are addicted and need help. 5

All over the world, there is evidence that Internet addiction is responsible for problems with school, work, and relationships. For that reason, South Korea is now testing schoolchildren for signs of Internet addiction. It is too late for Kim Kyung-jae and Lien Wen-cheng, but authorities hope that they can help other children of the cyber generation. If children show signs of Internet addiction, they will give them counseling. They will even hospitalize them if necessary. 6

Today, Jin is getting treatment that will help him. After his treatment, the Internet will continue to play a role in Jin's life, but a positive one. Jin is learning that too much time on the Internet is not good for you. 7

# 4 READING CHECK

**A** Circle the letter of the best answer for each question.

1 What were Kim and Lien doing online before they died?
   **a** studying     **b** working     **c** playing

2 What is a symptom of Internet Addiction Disorder?
   **a** spending time on the Internet
   **b** being unhappy when you are not on the Internet
   **c** having a job where you work on the Internet

3 Why are people worried about Internet use?
   **a** no one knows all the effects of long periods of Internet use
   **b** millions of young people may have IAD
   **c** both "a" and "b"

**B** Are these statements true or false? Write *T* (true) or *F* (false). Then correct any false statements.

1 _____ Kim Kyung-jae died after playing an online game for 8 days.

_____

2 _____ Kim and Lien died after spending many hours on the Internet.

_____

3 _____ Psychologists worry about the role the Internet plays in people's lives.

_____

4 _____ Jin's parents took away his computer because he did poorly on a test.

_____

5 _____ IAD is affecting 13.7 million young people in China.

_____

6 _____ The South Korean government does not consider Internet addiction a serious health issue.

_____

7 _____ Most people in South Korea have to go to a cyber café to use the Internet.

_____

8 _____ IAD treatment means that Jin will never use the computer again.

_____

## 5 VOCABULARY CHECK

**A** Retell the story. Fill in the blanks with the correct words from the box.

| | | | |
|---|---|---|---|
| access | addicted | authorities | collapsed |
| counseling | cyber café | disorder | estimate |
| generation | role | virtual reality | wired |

Kim Kyung-jae played a game online for so long that he
_____ and died. Lien Wen-cheng also died after he spent
1
36 hours playing an online game in a/an _____ . These
2
two men were _____ to online games, and they could not
3
stop playing. _____ in many countries are worried about
4
this. In China, experts in mental health have asked the government to
officially recognize Internet addiction as a/an _____ . They
5
_____ that it affects as many as 10 million young Chinese.
6
The experts are concerned about members of the _____
7
who have grown up in the age of the Internet. South Korean officials
are also worried. South Korea is one of the most _____
8
countries in the world. Ninety percent of households there have
_____ to high-speed Internet.
9

Being on the Internet can be a problem if people spend too much time
playing online games and get too involved in the _____
10
of the games. When the Internet plays too big a/an _____
11
in someone's life, it becomes a problem. At that point, the person probably
needs _____ .
12

**B** Some nouns and verbs often go together. Circle the verbs that often come
before the nouns in bold. More than one answer is possible.

| | | | | |
|---|---|---|---|---|
| **1** | treat | have | play | **a disorder** |
| **2** | be a member of | collapse | belong to | **a generation** |
| **3** | do | play | have | **a role** |
| **4** | develop | play | estimate | **a game** |
| **5** | get | make | provide | **counseling** |

## 6 APPLYING READING SKILLS

*Readings often include causes and effects. **Finding causes and effects** will help you understand a reading. Sometimes you can find a chain of causes and effects. In other words, one event causes another event that causes another event, and so on.*

**A** Read the list of events. Find the chain of causes and effects. Write the letter of each event in the diagram. The first cause is done for you.

**a** He spent 86 hours playing an online game.

**b** He died.

**c** A South Korean man was addicted to the Internet.

**d** People paid attention to this problem.

**e** He had heart failure.

**B** Practice finding causes and effects.

**1** Reread paragraph 4. Write a chain of cause-and-effect events that begins: *Jin got involved in an online game.*

**2** Reread paragraph 6. Write a chain of cause-and-effect events that begins: *Many South Korean schoolchildren show signs of Internet addiction.*

## 7 DISCUSSION

Discuss the following questions in pairs or groups.

**1** "Online games are addictive." Do you agree or disagree with this statement? Explain.

**2** Should parents limit the amount of time young people spend on the Internet? If so, how?

**3** Why do you think governments are worried about Internet Addiction Disorder? What can they do about it?

# 14
# The Power of the Mind

## 1 TOPIC PREVIEW

**A** Put a check (✓) next to the sentences that you agree with. Share your answers with your classmates.

**1** _____ If I think positive thoughts, I have a positive experience.

**2** _____ When I worry too much, I don't do well in sports or on tests.

**3** _____ I get very nervous before things like tests, presentations, or sports events.

**4** _____ I think about what I want to do, and then I focus completely on doing it.

**5** _____ I can focus totally on something and not pay attention to anything else.

**B** Read the title of this chapter, look at the picture, and discuss the following questions.

**1** What do you do to prepare your mind for things like tests?
**2** How do you think the power of the mind can help an athlete?
**3** What do you think the reading is going to be about?

## 2 VOCABULARY PREVIEW

**A** Read the word lists. Put a check (✓) next to the words that you know and can use in a sentence. Compare your answers with a partner. Then look up any unfamiliar words in a dictionary.

| Psychology | Academic Word List | Sports and Fitness |
|---|---|---|
| **block** (out) (*v.*) <br> **distraction** | **challenging** (*adj.*) <br> **concentration** <br> **mental** <br> **stress** (*n.*) | **dive** (into) (*v.*) <br> **exercise** (*n.*) <br> **fit** (*adj.*) <br> **stretch** (*v.*) <br> **tournament** <br> **work out** (*v.*) |

The chart shows selected words from the reading related to psychology, sports and fitness, and the Academic Word List (AWL). For more information about the AWL, see page 121.

**B** Fill in the blanks with words from Part A.

**1** How much _____ do people need to stay healthy?

**2** Does listening to music hurt your _____ , or does it help you study?

**3** The noise from the classroom next door was a/an _____ .

**4** She needs a vacation because she has had a lot of _____ lately.

**5** They competed in a golf _____ last week.

**6** He walks to work every day to stay _____ .

**7** Top athletes are in great shape physically, but they also need _____ strength.

**8** When students take tests, they need to _____ out all the noises and activity around them.

**9** It is dangerous to _____ into shallow water.

**10** The advanced course was very _____ , but the students did well.

**11** It is important to _____ before running or playing a sport.

**12** They _____ four times a week to stay in shape.

Preview the questions in Reading Check Part A on page 109. Then read the story.

# The Power of the Mind

World-famous golfer Tiger Woods is on the green[1] at the 18th hole. He gets ready to take his shot. Hundreds of people are watching, but that doesn't bother Woods. He makes the shot and wins the tournament.    1

What makes Woods a winner? As a young golfer, his mother introduced him to Buddhist philosophy. This helped him focus his mind on the moment. He learned to block out the crowds and the stress. When he was younger, his father often created distractions while Tiger was playing. He coughed or made sudden movements to test his son's concentration. Now many people say that it is Tiger's mental strength that helped him become the number one golfer in the world.    2

Lewis Gordon Pugh also knows a lot about the way the mind can control the body. Pugh is an ice swimmer from England. He swims in ice-cold water (32°F; 0°C) in just a regular bathing suit. He holds the world record for the longest cold-water swims in both the Arctic and Antarctic.    3

Pugh spends a great deal of time in mental preparation before each swim. Of course, he prepares his body, but more importantly, he prepares his mind. He often spends four hours a day thinking about challenging situations. He thinks about his reasons for wanting to break records. He thinks about every minute of the swim, imagining how it will feel in detail.    4

---

[1] *the green:* an area of smooth grass around a hole on a golf course

5    So far, he sounds like a normal athlete. What he does next, however, is extraordinary. He raises his body temperature by almost 3°F (1.4°C) to 101°F (38°C). He does it all by mental control. Then Pugh dives into the water. Most people would die in just a few minutes in the cold water. Their body temperature would drop to a dangerously low level. Pugh doesn't even shiver.[2] In the water, he can keep his body temperature at 96.8°F (36°C) for as long as 30 minutes. This is the time it takes him to complete a one-kilometer swim (about half a mile).

6    The ability of the mind to control the body is not only true for great athletes. Ellen Langer is a psychologist who is interested in the mind-body relationship. She studied hotel housekeepers who spent all day at work bending, stretching, and lifting. Langer asked them, "Are you physically active?" They said no, they did not get much exercise. Medical tests agreed. The housekeepers had the same physical health as office workers. This result did not make sense to Langer. The women were getting a lot of good exercise. Why weren't they showing any benefits?

7    Langer decided to do an experiment. She told half of the housekeepers that their jobs involved a lot of physical exercise. She told them that pushing a vacuum cleaner, changing sheets, and cleaning a bathroom required a lot of energy. She said these activities used the same amount of energy that people use when they work out at the gym. After a month, Langer retested all the women. This time, the results were different. Half of the housekeepers were thinner, fitter, and healthier. These were the housekeepers who thought they were working out. In fact, these housekeepers had not done anything differently. The only change was in their minds. They believed they were getting exercise. They believed they should get fitter and healthier. As soon as the housekeepers believed that, their bodies showed positive effects.

8    Tiger Woods, Lewis Gordon Pugh, and the housekeepers are all examples of the power of the mind and the mind's mysterious relationship to the body.

Lewis Gordon Pugh

---

[2] *shiver:*  shake slightly and quickly because a person feels cold

# 4 READING CHECK

**A** Match the people to the activity.

1 _____ Tiger Woods     **a** could control body temperature

2 _____ Lewis Gordon Pugh     **b** believed could lose weight, and did

3 _____ housekeepers     **c** could block out distractions

**B** Circle the letter of the best answer.

1 Tiger Woods first received mental training from _____ .
   **a** his parents     **b** his teacher     **c** other golfers

2 Woods's father helped his son become a great golfer by teaching him _____ .
   **a** Buddhist philosophy
   **b** to hit balls over the house
   **c** to block out distractions

3 Lewis Gordon Pugh is famous because he _____ .
   **a** is the youngest swimmer in England
   **b** won several Olympic medals in swimming
   **c** can swim in cold water longer than anyone else

4 How long can Pugh stay in freezing water?
   **a** 20 minutes
   **b** 30 minutes
   **c** 60 minutes

5 How does Pugh prepare for an ice swim?
   **a** He wears protective clothing.
   **b** He trains physically and mentally.
   **c** He eats and drinks only cold foods.

6 Who is Ellen Langer?
   **a** an athlete
   **b** a psychologist
   **c** a hotel housekeeper

7 One group of housekeepers did nothing different. The other group _____ .
   **a** did extra physical activity
   **b** was compared to office workers
   **c** learned that they were getting exercise

8 The housekeeper study showed the power of _____ .
   **a** staying fit     **b** the mind     **c** hard work

## 5 VOCABULARY CHECK

**A**  Retell the story. Fill in the blanks with the correct words from the box.

| | | | | |
|---|---|---|---|---|
| block out | challenging | concentration | distractions | dives |
| fitter | mental | stretching | tournaments | working out |

Sometimes, _____ preparation is just as important
1
as physical preparation. Tiger Woods is a great golfer partly because

he can ignore all _____ . This is important in
2

golf _____ , where crowds of people follow the
3

players and sometimes make noise. Tiger Woods, however, is able to

_____ everything but the game. _____
4                                               5

is also very important to Lewis Gordon Pugh. He is an ice swimmer who

prepares by imagining _____ situations. Before he
6

_____ into the freezing water, he focuses intensely and
7

raises his body temperature.

Mental control is not just helpful to great athletes. Hotel housekeepers

spend all day at work bending, _____ , and lifting. They
8

do not think of this as exercise. However, when housekeepers were told that

their work was similar to _____ at a gym, their bodies
9

changed. They became _____ just because they changed
10

the way they thought about their work.

**B**  Some words have the same form for the noun and the verb. How are the
underlined words used in the sentences? Circle *noun* or *verb*.

1  She is under a great deal of <u>stress</u> right now.     noun     verb

2  Where can we safely <u>dive</u>?     noun     verb

3  It is always hard to find the time to <u>exercise</u>.     noun     verb

4  <u>Exercise</u> is important for a healthy life.     noun     verb

5  You should always <u>stretch</u> before you run.     noun     verb

# 6 APPLYING READING SKILLS

*Each paragraph has a main idea. The main idea is what the paragraph is about.*
***Finding the main idea of a paragraph** is a key reading skill.*

**A** Look back at the reading, and find the correct paragraph for each main idea.

| MAIN IDEA | PARAGRAPH |
|---|---|
| Lewis Gordon Pugh is an outstanding ice swimmer. | |
| Ellen Langer was interested in why housekeepers were not more fit. | |
| Three examples show the mind-to-body relationship. | |

**B** Circle the letter of the best main idea for each paragraph.

**1** Paragraph 2
  **a** Tiger Woods's father created distractions to help Tiger prepare.
  **b** Tiger Woods's parents helped him develop mental focus.
  **c** Tiger Woods's parents both wanted him to play golf.

**2** Paragraph 4
  **a** Lewis Gordon Pugh prepares himself physically for the cold-water swim.
  **b** Lewis Gordon Pugh imagines how cold the water will be.
  **c** Lewis Gordon Pugh prepares mentally for his challenging swims.

**3** Paragraph 5
  **a** Pugh sounds like a normal athlete.
  **b** Pugh is able to control his body temperature.
  **c** Pugh dives into very cold water and doesn't even shiver.

**4** Paragraph 7
  **a** The housekeepers in the experiment worked very hard.
  **b** Langer's experiment showed that the mind can affect the body.
  **c** The housekeepers believed that they were getting a lot of exercise.

# 7 DISCUSSION

Discuss the following questions in pairs or groups.

**1** Sometimes top athletes lose to much less experienced athletes. Why do you think this happens?

**2** Do you believe that your mind can change your body physically? Explain.

**3** Do you think that the power of the mind can improve your health? Explain.

# Miracle on the Hudson

## 1 TOPIC PREVIEW

**A** Put a check (✓) next to the three qualities that you think are most important in an airplane pilot. Share your answers with your classmates.

**1** _____ good training

**2** _____ a lot of flying experience

**3** _____ perfect health

**4** _____ the ability to stay calm

**5** _____ _____ (your idea)

**B** Read the title of this chapter, look at the picture, and discuss the following questions.

**1** Do you think it is more dangerous in an emergency for a pilot to bring down a plane on water or on dry land? Explain.

**2** What does the word *miracle* mean? What do you think it means in the title?

**3** What do you think the reading is going to be about?

## 2 VOCABULARY PREVIEW

**A** Read the word lists. Put a check (✓) next to the words that you know and can use in a sentence. Compare your answers with a partner. Then look up any unfamiliar words in a dictionary.

| Psychology | Academic Word List | Aviation |
|---|---|---|
| anxious<br>crisis<br>panic (v.)<br>self-confidence | crucial<br>impact (n.)<br>option | casualty<br>cockpit<br>crew<br>landing (n.)<br>takeoff (n.) |

The chart shows selected words from the reading related to psychology, aviation, and the Academic Word List (AWL). For more information about the AWL, see page 121.

**B** Write the word from Part A next to its definition.

1 The physical force or action of one object hitting another:

   _____

2 When an aircraft leaves the ground and begins to fly: _____

3 A situation or time that is very difficult or dangerous: _____

4 The place where a pilot sits in an aircraft: _____

5 To suddenly feel so worried or frightened that you cannot think or behave calmly: _____

6 An arrival, usually of an aircraft: _____

7 Extremely important or necessary: _____

8 A choice: _____

9 Worried and nervous: _____

10 A group of people who work together, especially all those who work on and operate a ship or an aircraft: _____

11 A feeling of security about yourself and your abilities: _____

12 Someone who is injured or killed in an accident or war:

   _____

Preview the questions in Reading Check Part A on page 116. Then read the story.

# Miracle on the Hudson

1    Things were looking bad for Flight 1549 out of New York's LaGuardia Airport one cold winter day in 2009. At 3:24 p.m., just minutes after takeoff, the Airbus 320 flew straight into a flock[1] of large birds. There were several loud noises. Then both of the engines died. In the cockpit, Captain Chesley B. Sullenberger noticed a sharp smell of burning feathers[2] The plane was only 3,000 feet (914 meters) in the air, and it had no power. They were going down.

2    Behind Sullenberger in the cabin, 150 passengers knew they were in trouble. Many desperately turned on their cell phones to say good-bye to loved ones. Some on the plane cried, and others prayed, but Captain Sullenberger did not panic. The lives of the 150 passengers and five crew were in his hands. His ability to stay calm in the face of disaster was the only thing that could save them.

3    Sullenberger had 40 years of flying experience. Like many pilots, he had experience in the military, where he flew a fighter jet. Sullenberger was also a safety consultant[3] for airlines, so he knew a great deal about how to handle a crisis. He knew how to fly gliders,[4]

---

[1] *flock:* a group of birds

[2] *feathers:* the long, light objects that cover a bird's body

[3] *safety consultant:* a person who tells companies what they can do to make things less dangerous

[4] *glider:* an aircraft with no engine that flies by using its long wings to ride on air currents

too. This was a helpful skill because the jet was now behaving like a very heavy glider.

At first he thought he could turn the plane around for an emergency landing. However, the jet was right over the city. It was near too many tall buildings and "too low, too slow" to reach the airport. Then he thought he could probably fly across the Hudson River and land at a nearby airport in New Jersey. That wasn't a good idea, however. He might crash into a neighborhood full of people. 4

Sullenberger decided he had only one option. He would have to bring the plane down in the icy Hudson River. It was going to be a very difficult landing. A water landing is extremely unusual for a plane, especially a water landing with no casualties. He would need to keep the nose of the plane up and control the wings perfectly. If one wing went into the water, the plane would turn over and over. 5

Experts say that self-confidence is crucial when you have to act in a difficult situation. Captain Sullenberger was anxious, but he was confident. He believed he could land this plane. He did not panic. He brought the plane lower and lower. "Brace[5] for impact," he said over the intercom[6] At 3:31 p.m., the plane touched down on the water. There was a huge spray of water. The plane stopped, and it floated. 6

*Captain Sullenberger*

Sullenberger got up from his seat in the cockpit. He reached for the passenger list. As the passengers climbed out of the plane onto the wings, he checked off their names. Was everybody safe? 7

Outside the plane, it was only 20°F (-6.7°C), but the plane had landed in a busy part of the Hudson River. Ferries, rescue boats, and helicopters came close to the plane and started rescuing passengers. Captain Sullenberger went back inside. One last time, he walked through the plane to make sure everyone was off. In the end, all 155 people on board Flight 1549 survived. People called it a miracle. The miracle was that they had the right captain at the right time. 8

---

[5] *brace:* to prepare your body for something unpleasant

[6] *intercom:* a system that allows the captain in the cockpit to communicate with the passengers

## 4 READING CHECK

**A** Are these statements true or false? Write *T* (true) or *F* (false).

1 _____ Flight 1549 was flying in an area with few people or houses.

2 _____ Captain Sullenberger landed the airplane on a river.

3 _____ Everyone survived the landing.

**B** Circle the letter of the best answer.

1 What caused Flight 1549's problem?
   **a** an engine fire      **b** flock of birds      **c** low fuel

2 How many passengers and crew were on board?
   **a** 40      **b** 150      **c** 155

3 While the plane was going down, it _____ .
   **a** was on fire      **b** acted like a glider      **c** lost a wing

4 Why couldn't Captain Sullenberger turn the plane around?
   **a** He did not have enough fuel to go back to the airport.
   **b** The airport was too crowded with other planes waiting to land.
   **c** His plane was too close to the ground and did not have enough speed.

5 Which statement is *not* true about Captain Sullenberger?
   **a** He was sure about his ability to land the plane.
   **b** He was calm in the face of disaster.
   **c** He could not decide what to do.

6 How much time passed between hitting the birds and landing the plane?
   **a** 7 minutes
   **b** 24 minutes
   **c** 31 minutes

7 What did Sullenberger do after the plane was on the water?
   **a** He radioed for help.
   **b** He used the intercom to tell the passengers to get out of the plane.
   **c** He used his passenger list to check that everyone was safely outside.

8 What happened to the passengers after they left the plane?
   **a** They swam across the river to safety.
   **b** Emergency aircraft and boats rescued them.
   **c** They used the life rafts on the plane to get to land.

# 5 VOCABULARY CHECK

**A** Retell the story. Fill in the blanks with the correct words from the box.

| | | | |
|---|---|---|---|
| anxious | casualties | cockpit | crew |
| crisis | crucial | impact | landing |
| options | panic | self-confidence | takeoff |

Minutes after _____ , Flight 1549 flew into a flock
of birds, and the engines failed. Captain Sullenberger faced a/an
_____ . His decisions in this situation were
_____ to the lives of 155 people, including his own.
Although Sullenberger was _____ , he stayed calm.
He considered making an emergency _____ in New Jersey.
However, that might cause more _____ if the plane crashed
into houses on the ground. Sullenberger did not _____ .
After considering all his _____ , he decided to land in
the Hudson River. He told everyone to brace for _____ .
Sullenberger's experience and _____ helped him land the
jet safely in the Hudson. Everyone survived. The passengers and
_____ on Flight 1549 were lucky that Sullenberger was
in the airplane's _____ that day.

**B** Write each word from the box in the correct category below.

| | | | |
|---|---|---|---|
| anxious | cockpit | crew | landing |
| panic | self-confidence | takeoff | |

| RELATED TO AIRPLANES | RELATED TO EMOTIONS |
|---|---|
| | |

## 6 APPLYING READING SKILLS

*Your reading speed is the number of words you can read per minute.*
***Increasing your reading speed*** *will make it easier to do all the reading for your classes. Timing yourself when you read will help you read faster.*

**A** Reread "Miracle on the Hudson" on page 114, and time yourself. Write your starting time, your finishing time, and the number of minutes it took you to read. Then calculate your reading speed.

> **Story title:** "Miracle on the Hudson" (560 words)
> Starting time: _____
> Finishing time: _____
> Total reading time: _____ minutes
> *Reading speed: _____ words per minute

*To calculate your reading speed, divide the number of words in the text (560) by your total reading time (the number of minutes you needed to read the text).

**B** Now reread either "Death by Internet" (562 words) on page 100 or "The Power of the Mind" (594 words) on page 107. Time yourself. Write the title of the story and your times below. Then calculate your reading speed.

> **Story title:** _____ ( _____ words)
> Starting time: _____
> Finishing time: _____
> Total reading time: _____ minutes
> Reading speed: _____ words per minute

## 7 DISCUSSION

Discuss the following questions in pairs or groups.

1 Why do people call the survival of all the passengers and crew on Flight 1549 a miracle? What things made this "miracle" possible?

2 Have you ever seen a movie about a dangerous situation in a plane? If so, what happened?

3 Which do you think is safer: traveling by car or traveling by plane? Explain.

## VOCABULARY REVIEW

| Chapter **13** | Chapter **14** | Chapter **15** |
|---|---|---|
| **Psychology** | **Psychology** | **Psychology** |
| **addicted** (to) · **counseling** · **disorder** | **block** (out) (*v.*) · **distraction** | **anxious** · **crisis** · **panic** (*v.*) · **self-confidence** |
| **Academic Word List** | **Academic Word List** | **Academic Word List** |
| (have) **access** (to) · **authority** · **collapse** (*v.*) · **estimate** (*v.*) · **generation** · **role** | **challenging** (*adj.*) · **concentration** · **mental** · **stress** (*n.*) | **crucial** · **impact** (*n.*) · **option** |
| **Technology** | **Sports and Fitness** | **Aviation** |
| **cyber café** · **virtual reality** · **wired** | **dive** (into) (*v.*) · **exercise** (*n.*) · **fit** (*adj.*) · **stretch** (*v.*) · **tournament** · **work out** (*v.*) | **casualty** · **cockpit** · **crew** · **landing** (*n.*) · **takeoff** (*n.*) |

Find words in the chart that match the definitions. Answers to 1–4 are from Chapter 13. Answers to 5–8 are from Chapter 14. Answers to 9–12 are from Chapter 15.

**1** Images and sounds produced on a computer that seem real: _____

**2** Having a need or strong desire to do or to have something: _____

**3** To fall down suddenly: _____

**4** A person with official responsibilities: _____

**5** Of or about the mind; involving the process of thinking: _____

**6** A competition with many competitors in one sport or game: _____

**7** To become longer or to reach across a distance: _____

**8** To stop something from being received: _____

**9** To feel so worried or frightened that you cannot be calm: _____

**10** A situation or time that is very difficult or dangerous: _____

**11** An arrival, usually of an aircraft or a boat: _____

**12** A choice: _____

## VOCABULARY IN USE

Work with a partner or small group, and discuss the questions below.

1 Do you go to **cyber cafés**? Why or why not?

2 Does your **generation** use technology differently from your parents? Explain.

3 What kinds of **exercise** do you enjoy?

4 What can a person do to reduce **stress**?

5 What is the most **challenging** thing you have ever done? Explain.

6 What **distractions** are most dangerous for a person driving a car?

7 Do you think it is possible to have too much **self-confidence**? Explain.

8 What things do you think are **crucial** to being successful in life? Explain.

## ROLE PLAY

Work with a partner. Student A is a psychologist. Student B is one of the characters below. Student B should talk about his or her experiences. The psychologist should ask questions and give advice. When you finish, change roles. This time, choose a different character.

- **A young person who is addicted to video games**

- **An athlete who wants to improve his or her performance in a sport**

- **A passenger who had a scary experience and is now afraid of flying**

## WRITING

Imagine you write an advice column in a newspaper. Answer one of the letters below, and give the person advice.

- I think I am addicted to video games. My grades are bad, and my parents are angry, but I can't stop my need to play. Please help.

- I am a (tennis player / swimmer / basketball player / other sport). I think I have good skills, but when I'm nervous, I don't do well. What should I do?

- I often have to fly on business, but I feel worried when I fly in bad weather. What can I do to control my anxiety?

## WEBQUEST

Find more information about the topics in this unit by going on the Internet. Go to www.cambridge.org/readthis and follow the instructions for doing a WebQuest. Search for facts. Have fun. Good luck!

# The Academic Word List

What are the most common words in academic English? Which words appear most frequently in readings in different academic subject areas? Dr. Averil Coxhead, who is currently a Senior Lecturer at Victoria University of Wellington in New Zealand, did research to try to answer these questions. The result was the Academic Word List (AWL).

Coxhead studied readings in English from many different academic fields. She found 570 words or word families that appear in many of those readings. These are words like *estimate* and *estimation*; *analyze*, *analysis*, and *analytical*; *evident*, *evidence*, and *evidently* – words that you can expect to find when reading a sociology text, a computer science text, or even a music studies text. So if you want to read nonfiction in English or academic English, these are the words that are going to be most useful for you to study and learn.

When you study the readings in *Read This!*, you will study words that belong to two different academic subject areas. These words will help you understand the topic of each reading. In addition, you will study AWL words in the readings. Learning the AWL words will help you, not just when you are reading on that topic, but when you read any academic text, because these words are likely to come up in your reading again and again.

In the list below, we show you all the words that are from the Academic Word List that are in all three books of the *Read This!* series. Many of these words appear in several of the readings. However, the words in the list that are followed by letters and numbers are words that are the focus of study in one of the readings. The letters and numbers show which book and chapter the word appears in. For example, "access RT2, 13" tells you that you study the word *access* in *Read This!* Book 2, Chapter 13. When the letters and numbers after the word appear in color, that tells you that the word is the focus of study in this *Read This!* book.

From time to time you might want to study the words in this list and test yourself. By going to the chapter where the word appears, you can see the words in context, which is one of the best ways to study new or unfamiliar words.

The following list shows the AWL words that appear in the *Read This!* series.

## A

access RT2, 13
accurate
accurately RT2, 6
achieve
achievement RT1, 5
adjust RT3, 14
adult RT2, 12
affect RT3, 11
alternative
analysis RT2, 12; RT3, 13
analyze
appreciate RT3, 1
approach RT3, 1
approaching
approximately RT1, 13
area RT1, 3
assist RT2, 5
assistance
authority RT2, 13
available
aware
awareness RT3, 8

## B

beneficial
benefit RT2, 9

## C

challenge RT1, 7; RT2, 2;
   RT3, 3
challenged
challenging RT2, 14
channel
chapter

chemical RT3, 5
civil
classical
coincidence RT1, 9
collapse RT2, 13
comment
commit
communicate RT1, 1
communication
compensation
complex RT3, 4
computer
concentrate RT3, 14
concentration RT2, 14
conduct
conflict RT3, 10
constant
construct RT3, 1
construction
consultant
consume RT2, 9
contact RT3, 4
contrast
contribute
contribution RT1, 7
controversial RT3, 11
conventional RT3, 7
couple
create RT1, 3
creative RT2, 4
crucial RT2, 15
cultural
culture
cycle RT3, 6

## D

data RT2, 9
define
design RT1, 14; RT3, 3
designer
detect RT2, 6
device RT3, 9
discriminate
discrimination
display RT3, 10
disposable RT3, 5
distinct RT3, 2
distinction
distinctive
distinctly
diverse RT3, 2
document RT3, 10
documented
domain

## E

energy RT1, 15
enormous RT1, 10
environment
environmental
environmentally
equipment RT3, 8
establish RT3, 6
estate
estimate RT2, 13
eventually
evidence RT2, 12; RT3, 12
evolve RT3, 15
exhibit RT3, 11

expand RT2, 7

expert RT1, 2; RT2, 10; RT3, 5

export RT1, 12

# F

feature RT1, 8

federal

federations

fee

file RT1, 5

final

finally

flexibility RT3, 9

flexible

focus RT1, 6

foundation RT3, 3

function RT1, 8

# G

generation RT2, 13; RT3, 15

global RT1, 10

goal RT3, 8

grade

guideline RT1, 8

# H

highlight

# I

identical RT2, 11

identification RT3, 13

identified

identify RT2, 6

identifying

identity RT2, 10

illegal RT3, 12

image RT2, 4

impact RT2, 15

individual RT3, 7

injure

injured

injury RT3, 9

institute RT2, 4

instructions

intelligence

intelligent

intense RT3, 6

interaction RT3, 2

interactive

investigate RT2, 11; RT3, 12

investigating

investigation

investigative

investigator

investor

involve

isolate RT2, 8

issue

item

# J

job

# L

layer RT3, 3

legal

liberate RT3, 11

locate

location

# M

maintain RT2, 5

major

maximum RT3, 14

media

medical

mental RT2, 14; RT3, 8

method RT2, 2

military

monitor RT3, 4

# N

network RT1, 5

normal RT2, 3

normally RT1, 1

# O

obviously RT2, 10

occur RT2, 8

option RT2, 15

# P

participate RT1, 4

participation RT3, 7

partner RT1, 2

percent

period

philosophy

physical RT2, 8; RT3, 8

physically

policy RT3, 10

positive

predict RT1, 11; RT2, 6; RT3, 1

prime

principle RT3, 10

procedure RT2, 3

process RT2, 9; RT3, 5

project RT1, 5; RT3, 3

promote

psychological

psychologist

psychology

publish RT3, 12

publisher RT1, 4

publishing

purchase

## R

range

ratio RT1, 8

reaction RT3, 11

recover RT2, 3

recovered

recovery RT3, 9

region RT3, 5

register RT1, 11

registration

relax

release RT3, 4

reluctant RT3, 2

rely

remove

require RT3, 13

research RT1, 1

researcher RT2, 1

resource

respond RT1, 7; RT2, 8

response

restrict RT2, 9

restricted

restricting

restriction

reveal RT3, 5

role RT2, 13

route RT3, 14

## S

section

security RT1, 2

sequence RT1, 9

shift RT3, 15

significant RT3, 2

significantly RT2, 9

similar RT2, 1

similarity RT1, 9

site RT2, 6

source RT1, 15; RT2, 7; RT3, 12

specific RT1, 14

specifically RT3, 9

specification

specify

stability RT3, 10

stabilize

stable

strategy RT1, 12

stress RT2, 14

structure RT1, 13; RT2, 4; RT3, 3

style RT1, 4; RT3, 15

survey RT3, 4

survive RT2, 3; RT3, 6

survivor

sustainable

symbol RT1, 3; RT2, 7; RT3, 11

## T

tape RT1, 6

task

team

technology

theory RT2, 2

trace

tradition

traditional RT3, 2

traditionally

transit

transition RT3, 15

transport RT2, 5; RT3, 13

## U

uniform

unique RT1, 14; RT2, 11; RT3, 1

## V

vehicle RT3, 13

virtual

volunteer RT1, 15

# Art Credits